The Truly Healthy Chili Cookbook

The Ultimate Guide To Easy and Delicious Chili Recipes You Can Make With One Pot To Maintain A Healthy Weight Without Skimping On Flavor

Richard Tillcot

LET'S START!

Table Of Contents

10 Reasons to love chili

144 Delicious Recipes

Spicy Pumpkin Chili 18

Green Chili Quiche Squares 19

Chili Rubbed Pork Tenderloin With Apricot Ginger 19

Gramma's Old Fashioned Chili Mac 20

Thirty Minute Chili 20

Daddy's 'If They'da had This at the Alamo we 21

White Chili IV 23

Ham and Bean Chili 24

Massachusetts Straub Chili 25

Chili Cheese Dip II 25

Insanely Easy Vegetarian Chili 26

Chili con Carne III 26

Fifteen Minute Chicken Chili 27

Chicken Chili I 28

Quick Chili I 28

Smokin' Scovilles Turkey Chili 29

Best Ever Chuck Wagon Chili 30

Nina's Texas Chili...30

It's Chili by George!! 31

Chili Colorado 32

Jim Kaczmarek's Chili 32

Skyline Chili I 33

Darn Good Chili 33

Baked Snapper with Chilies, Ginger and Basil..34

Stove Top Tofu Chili 35

White Chili II...35

Cheddar Chili Braid..36

Texas Deer Chili..36

White Chicken Chili..37

Mr. Bill's New Mexico Buffalo Chili...37

Chili con Carne I...38

White Bean Chicken Chili...39

Chuck's Come On Ice Cream (or Night of the Red......................................39

Chili Dog Casserole I...40

Bob Evans® Favorite Chili Recipe...41

Wazzu Tailgate Chili...41

Chili Cheese Fries...42

Maverick Moose Chili..42

Southwestern Three-Meat Chili..43

Black Bean and Chickpea Chili...44

Chili-Lime Chicken Kabobs..45

Aush (Afghani Chili)..45

Chili Chops..46

Chili-Stuffed Peppers..47

Chili-Cheese Spoon Bread...47

Chili Corn Bread Wedges...48

Speedy Chili Mac..49

Pressure Cooker Chili..49

Coriander and Chili Almonds..50

Polish Chili..51

Slow-Cooked White Chili...51

White Chili with Ground Turkey..52

Cincinnati Skyline Chili...53

Sausage Corn Chili...53

Rotisserie Chicken Chili With Hominy & Chiles...54

Smokin' Texas Chili...55

Chili Barbecue Chops..55

Penne with Chili, Chicken, and Prawns...56

Easy Homemade Chili...56

Carol's Chicken Chili...57

Chili Cups...57

Butternut Squash and Turkey Chili...58

Chili Bean Nacho Skillet...58

Kas' Chili...59

Venison Tequila Chili...59

Buffalo Chicken Chili...60

Belly Burner Chili...61

Dad's Chili...61

Chili Mac...62

Chili Jack Chicken...62

Cheesy Green Chili Rice...63

Mexican Chocolate Chili...63

Spicy Chili Seasoning Mix...64

Easy Texas Chili...64

Authentic Cincinnati Chili...66

Paprika Chili Steak...66

Shrimp Lollipops with Pineapple Chili Dipping...67

Chili Cheese Snacks...68

Potatoes with Fresh Ginger and Chilies...68

Golden Chili Chicken...68

Chili For Two...69

Nacho Chili...70

Vegetarian Black Bean Chili...70

Beef, Green Chili and Tomato Stew...71

Colorado Green Chili (Chile Verde)...72

Chili II...73

Corn with Bacon and Chili Powder...73

The Best Vegetarian Chili in the World...74

Pinto Bean Chili 75

Boilermaker Tailgate Chili 75

Bold Vegan Chili 77

DB's Seven Pepper Chili 77

Chili Chicken I 78

Chili IV 79

West Texas-Style Buffalo Chili 79

Unbelievably Easy and Delicious Vegetarian Chili 80

Slow Cooker Sweet Chicken Chili 80

Carne Con Chilies 81

Chili Stew 82

Chili Casserole 82

Sharon's Awesome Chicago Chili 83

Green Enchilada Pork Chili 83

Cincinnati Chili I 84

Corn Chili 85

Best Yet Turkey Chili 86

Taste of Home's Double Chili Cheese Dip 86

Green Chili Casserole 87

Vegetarian Chili 87

Chili Casserole 88

Chili Cheese Dip III 88

Diann's Chili Vegetable Soup 89

Amateur's Light Breeze Chicken Chili 89

Quick Zesty Chili 90

Lentil Chili 90

Portobello Mushroom Chili 90

Kelly's Chili 91

Ken's Texas Chili 92

Dorm Room Chili Mac 92

Microwave Classic Chili 93

Habanero Hellfire Chili 93

Venison Chili 94

Wagon Wheel Chili 95

Chili Cheese Soup 95

Three-Bean Chili 96

Mom's Chili 96

Chili Chops 97

Chili Seasoning Mix II 97

Chili Popcorn 98

Pumpkin Chili 98

Grandma's Slow Cooker Vegetarian Chili 99

Chili Cheese Grits 99

Bewitching Chili 100

Josh's Four-Way Chili 100

Smoky Chipotle Chili 101

Cincinnati Chili II 102

Chili Relleno Squares 102

Green Chili Burritos 103

The Ultimate Chili 103

Drunk Deer Chili 104

Frank's Spicy Alabama Onion Beer Chili 104

Chili-Stuffed Baked Potatoes 105

Turkey Bean Chili 106

Dakota's Texas Style Chili 107

Chili-Spiced Chicken Breasts 107

10 Reasons to love chili

Winter is the season for comfort, happiness and family. It lets us take advantage of the fresh air and all sorts of outdoor activities like skating, skiing, sledding, snowshoeing, etc. When we come in and warm up after a good day of winter sports, the desire for warmth often makes us want to prepare meals that reinvigorate and comfort us. For starters, chili con carne was a dish originally made with ground or minced beef (hence con carne which means meat) and chili peppers which are very spicy. To that, a Mexican spice blend made up of hot peppers, paprika, garlic, cumin, etc. is added. In its more contemporary version, chili has tomatoes, onion, garlic and sometimes bell peppers, beans, corn kernels, coriander and several other ingredients. Very popular in many countries and cooked in as many different variations, this dish has countless secrets we don't know about. Let's discover them together.

The Controversial origins of chili con carne

Where does chili con carne really come from? Most people would probably say, "Mexico, of course!" Surprisingly, they would be wrong. Although the exact origins are not known for sure, this dish is without a doubt the signature of the southern United States, just as shepherd's pie is for Québec. Some joke about the famous Quebec steak, corn on the cob and potatoes, but chili con carne isn't that much more refined because it actually means "peppers with meat".

Chili specialists have a few theories about the creation of the dish, each one just as plausible as the next, so here are two versions that Texans most believe are the origins: Created in San Antonio, Texas, at the beginning of the 19th century, it was initially just a simple stew  with chili peppers sold by chili queens who were, in fact, women who cooked huge quantities of chili at home before going to the public market to sell individual portions at a lower cost. Texan prisoners would have had the chance to eat chili practically every day as this dish was not very expensive. Some of them recreated the dish once they left prison and it became really popular! Even though the exact origins of this dish remains a mystery, one thing is for sure: with its Mexican-sounding name, chili con carne is a typical Tex-Mex dish. In other words, it means that it may be found at the heart of Texas, but its inspiration is Mexican!

Chili cook-offs Craze!

The world of chili cook-offs aren't really well known here in Canada. There really are cooking competitions that showcase chili where participants cook their dishes right at the event site. These contests happen across the United States, but mainly in Texas where the first ones took place. Since 1970, the Chili Appreciation Society International has been organizing the annual World Open Chili Championship in Tarlingua, Texas. For the Society, these competitions serve to raise money for charitable work while participants cease the opportunity to stand out with their original chili recipe and maybe win a prize or simply bragging rights! Every year, hundreds if not thousands of people go there to watch or participate in one or several chili cook-offs. The contests are open to everyone, but participants must go through a qualification process in order to get to the international championship. Also, these competitions are governed by several regulations like not being allowed to cook under a shelter or use certain ingredients that stray too far from the original recipe. Finally, winners are chosen after several rounds of criteria relating to things like the food's taste and after-taste, as well as its appearance (consistency and colour). Who knows? Maybe these contests will make it to Canada one day so that we can then participate!

February 26: National Chili Day

Surprisingly, National Chili Day is celebrated every year on the 4th Thursday of February. This is the perfect dish to cook to boost the troops' moral at the end of one of the coldest months in winter. It will be celebrated very soon this year – on Thursday, February 26! Mark the date on your calendar now because you know what you'll make that night!

10 Reasons to love chili

1. First and foremost – health

Chili can be really healthy if the cook wants it to be. Adding onions, two kinds of bell peppers and corn kernels makes chili chocked full of nutrients and vitamins. You can put whatever veggies you like – carrots, celery, zucchini, etc.

2. Chili savings

Did you know that a serving of chili costs around $1.50 or $2 depending on the recipe? Ingredients like paprika, chili powder and cumin can be used for other recipes, so you don't need to buy them every time you make a chili. For veggies, use whatever you have lying around the fridge and that are ready to be cooked. Ground beef is definitely the most expensive ingredient in this recipe, but you can put less if you want the dish to be as affordable as possible!

3. Three words: Practical, simple, quick

Some chili recipes are complicated and take time to prepare. The beauty of this dish is that there are many tasty recipes that take 10-15 minutes to prepare and 30 minutes to cook. It's simple. You just have to put all of your ingredients in a big pot and let the whole thing simmer while you take care of other things, like laundry or homework with the kids.

4. No one will be left hungry

Chili is known to be filling. After eating a serving, kids won't ask for anything else the rest of the night because they'll be really full. The combination of red kidney beans, tomato sauce, ground beef and veggies will tide everyone over whether they have big appetites or small ones!

5. When the chili comes, let the festivities begin!

What better to make than a hearty chili with tortillas or nachos when friends come over? Whether it's a potluck or snack before a football or hockey game, chili is sure to be a crowd pleaser and will add spice to your tailgate party, especially if you make a spicy recipe!

6. Leftovers aren't lost

As mentioned earlier, there are many recipes perfect for your leftover chili. If you don't think you'll eat the leftovers before they go bad, freeze some of it. It'll definitely be a lifesaver one night when you have many mouths to feed, but little time to get something on the table.

7. Kids approve!

Several chili recipes have been tested on kids and they definitely approve of the dish. If your kids are a little pickier and your recipe has an ingredient they don't like, try replacing it and you'll see how much they'll love the reinvented version made specially for them! If they're still sceptical, have them help prepare the meal with you. They'll suddenly enjoy the dish a lot more.

8. Versatility at its best

Without a doubt, chili can be cooked in every way possible! It doesn't matter what your favourite food is and what's in the fridge, there's a recipe right for you. In the mood for something sweet? Simply swap out cumin and paprika for honey or maple syrup. Got a roast pork to cook? Cut it into small pieces and add it to your chili. In short, whatever situation presents itself, making chili is always an option.

9. Chili sin carne: Your veggie dish of the week

Many people opt for a few meatless meals during the week, but have trouble finding dishes that have enough substance and protein. Chili sin carne with red kidney beans and/or chick peas is the ideal dish for this kind of meal! Take advantage to double the amount of veggies in your recipe. You'll love it!

10. All in one!

Once prepared, chili is a dish that is satisfying in itself! No need to make side dishes like rice or sautéed veggies because you'll find all the nutrients you need in the same mouthful. And you don't have to dirty several pots and serving dishes because one is all that's needed. Variations of the recipe. Since its creation, the chili recipe has evolved according to the various regions where it's made. In the northern US, corn kernels are added whereas in the east, it's cheese that completes the dish.

In Canada, red kidney beans are served with it which is considered a sacrilege by Texans! Ingredients that seem to be found in the dish regardless of the region are onions, garlic, tomatoes, chili powder, cumin, coriander and peppers. The most popular is still chili con carne although there is a version called sin carne or non carne meaning without meat. The word chili (which right away means there are chili peppers in the recipe), is now used throughout the world and indicates that the dish uses it whether it's vegetarian or not.

144 DELICIOUS RECIPES

Spicy Pumpkin Chili

Ingredients	Directions
<ul><li>1 pound ground beef</li><li>1/2 teaspoon crushed red pepper flakes, or to taste</li><li>1 teaspoon minced garlic</li><li>1/2 large onion, diced</li><li>1 green bell pepper, chopped</li><li>1 red bell pepper, chopped</li><li>1 (15 ounce) can kidney beans, rinsed and drained</li><li>1 (15 ounce) can black beans, rinsed and drained</li><li>1 (15 ounce) can Great Northern beans, drained and rinsed</li><li>1 (8 ounce) can tomato sauce</li><li>1 (4 ounce) can tomato sauce with garlic and onions</li><li>2 (14.5 ounce) cans petite diced tomatoes</li><li>1 (14.5 ounce) can fire roasted diced tomatoes</li><li>1 (15 ounce) can pumpkin puree</li><li>2 teaspoons pumpkin pie spice</li><li>2 teaspoons chili powder</li><li>1 teaspoon ground cumin</li><li>1 teaspoon salt, or to taste</li></ul>	Heat a large skillet over medium-high heat; cook and stir the beef in the skillet until crumbly and no longer pink, about 5 minutes. Stir in the red pepper flakes, garlic, and onion; continue cooking until the beef has browned and the onion has softened and turned translucent. Add the green and red bell pepper and cook 5 minutes more. While the beef is cooking, combine the kidney beans, black beans, Great Northern beans, tomato sauce, tomato sauce with garlic and onions, petite diced tomatoes, fire roasted diced tomatoes, and pumpkin puree in a large slow cooker. Season with pumpkin pie spice, chili powder, cumin, and salt. Stir in the ground beef mixture. Cook on Low until the chili is hot, 1 to 2 hours.

Green Chili Quiche Squares

Ingredients	Directions
❖ 3 cups seasoned croutons ❖ 1 (4 ounce) can chopped green chilies ❖ 4 cups shredded Cheddar cheese ❖ 6 eggs ❖ 3 cups milk ❖ 2 teaspoons ground mustard ❖ 1 teaspoon salt ❖ 1/4 teaspoon garlic powder	Arrange croutons in a greased 13-in. x 9-in. x 2-in. baking dish. Sprinkle with chilies and cheese. In a bowl, beat the eggs, milk, mustard, salt and garlic powder. Pour over cheese. Cover and refrigerate for 8 hours or overnight. Remove from the refrigerator 30 minutes before baking. Bake, uncovered, at 350 degrees F for 40-45 minutes or until a knife inserted near the center comes out clean. Let stand for 10 minutes before cutting.

Chili Rubbed Pork Tenderloin With Apricot Ginger

Ingredients	Directions
❖ 2 (1 pound) pork tenderloins, trimmed Spice Rub: ❖ 1 tablespoon chili powder ❖ 1 tablespoon garlic powder 1/2 tablespoon sugar ❖ 1 teaspoon salt ❖ 1/2 teaspoon ground black pepper Glaze: ❖ 1 1/2 cups apricot preserves ❖ 1/2 cup barbecue sauce ❖ 1 teaspoon grated ginger ❖ 1/2 teaspoon garlic powder ❖ 1/2 teaspoon hot sauce ❖ 1 tablespoon chopped cilantro ❖ 1 lime, juiced	Place chili powder, garlic powder, sugar, salt and pepper in a jar; shake to blend. Rub spice mixture onto pork tenderloins. Cover tenderloins and refrigerate for 2 to 24 hours. Prior to grilling, melt apricot preserves in saucepan over medium heat. Remove pan from the heat and stir in remaining glaze ingredients. Place half of the glaze in a serving bowl and hold for service. Prepare grill at medium-high heat. Grill pork tenderloins for 15-20 minutes, or until the internal temperature of the pork reaches 160 degrees F. on an instant-read thermometer. When approximately 4 minutes of cook time remains, brush the pork tenderloins with the apricot glaze remaining in the

pan. Cook for 2 minutes, turn the pork tenderloins and brush glaze on other side. Cook for an additional 2 minutes. Remove pork from the grill and let set for about 5 minutes before slicing. Serve with reserved glaze.

Gramma's Old Fashioned Chili Mac

Ingredients	Directions
❖ 1 cup elbow macaroni ❖ 1 pound ground beef ❖ 1 small onion, chopped ❖ 1 cup chopped celery ❖ 1/2 large green bell pepper, chopped ❖ 1 (15 ounce) can kidney beans, drained ❖ 2 (10.75 ounce) cans condensed tomato soup ❖ 2 (14.5 ounce) cans diced tomatoes ❖ 1/8 cup brown sugar salt and pepper to taste	Bring a pot of lightly salted water to a boil. Add pasta and cook for 8 to 10 minutes or until al dente; drain. In a small saucepan, simmer celery and green pepper with water to cover until tender; Drain. Place ground beef in a large heavy skillet over medium heat. Cook until evenly brown. Add onion, and cook until tender and translucent. Drain excess fat. Add celery and green pepper. Stir in kidney beans, condensed tomato soup, diced tomatoes and brown sugar. Season with salt and pepper, and stir in macaroni.

Thirty Minute Chili

Ingredients	Directions
❖ 1 pound ground beef ❖ 1 (14.5 ounce) can canned diced tomatoes ❖ 1 (15 ounce) can kidney beans, drained ❖ 1 (1.25 ounce) package chili seasoning mix	Crumble the beef into a large skillet over medium-high heat. Cook and stir until evenly browned. Drain off grease, and mix in the tomatoes, kidney beans and chili seasoning mix. Reduce heat to medium, and simmer for 15 minutes.

Daddy's 'If They'da had This at the Alamo we

Ingredients	Directions
❖ 3 tablespoons bacon drippings ❖ 2 large onions, chopped ❖ 8 pounds beef stew meat, or coarse ground chili beef ❖ 5 cloves garlic, finely chopped ❖ 4 tablespoons ground red chile pepper ❖ 4 tablespoons mild chili powder ❖ 1 tablespoon ground cumin ❖ 1/4 cup sweet Hungarian paprika ❖ 1 teaspoon dried Mexican oregano ❖ 3 (10 ounce) cans tomato sauce ❖ 1 (6 ounce) can tomato paste ❖ 3 cups water ❖ 2 tablespoons salt ❖ 1/4 cup dried parsley (optional) ❖ 1 fresh jalapeno peppers ❖ 1 cup masa harina flour	Melt the bacon drippings in a large heavy pot over medium heat. Add the onions and cook until they are translucent. Combine the beef with the garlic, ground chile, chili powder and cumin. Add this meat-and-spices to the onions in the pot. Break up any meat that sticks together as you cook, stirring occasionally, about 30 minutes, until meat is evenly browned (very browned, not just gray). Sprinkle in Hungarian paprika and oregano. Pour in the tomato sauce, tomato paste, water, salt, parsley and jalapeno. Bring to a boil, then lower the heat and simmer, uncovered, for 1 hour. NOTE: True Texans DO NOT add beans to their chili, but my husband loves them, so this is the point where you can add as many cans of drained and rinsed pinto beans as you wish (I add 2 cans, but shhhhhh don't tell my Daddy!!!). During cooking you may squeeze the jalapeno as it softens against the sides of the pot to release more heat if desired. Mix in the masa harina, and cook while stirring for 30 minutes longer, or until desired consistency is achieved. Taste and adjust seasonings.

White Chili IV

Ingredients	Directions
❖ 1 tablespoon olive oil ❖ 4 skinless, boneless chicken breast halves - cubed ❖ coarsely ground black pepper to taste ❖ 1 large onion, chopped ❖ 6 cloves garlic, minced ❖ 3 green chile peppers, seeded and minced ❖ 1 green bell pepper, chopped ❖ 1 red bell pepper, chopped ❖ 1 (8 ounce) package mushrooms, sliced ❖ 3 (15 ounce) cans pinto beans ❖ 4 green onions, chopped ❖ 1 bunch fresh parsley, chopped ❖ 1 cup white wine ❖ 2 (14.5 ounce) cans chicken broth ❖ 2 cubes chicken bouillon ❖ 1 teaspoon dried rosemary ❖ 1 teaspoon dried thyme ❖ 1 tablespoon dried oregano ❖ 1 1/2 tablespoons ground cumin ❖ 2 bay leaves	In a large pot over medium-high heat, cook chicken in olive oil with black pepper until brown. Stir in onion, garlic and chiles and cook until onion begins to soften. Stir in bell peppers, mushrooms, beans, green onions and parsley. Pour in wine and chicken broth. Season with bouillon, rosemary, thyme, oregano and cumin. Place bay leaves in pot, cover, reduce heat and simmer 90 minutes

Ham and Bean Chili

Ingredients	Directions
❖ 2 cups cubed fully cooked ham ❖ 1 medium onion, chopped ❖ 1 medium green pepper, chopped ❖ 1 garlic clove, minced ❖ 1 tablespoon olive or vegetable oil ❖ 1 (28 ounce) can diced tomatoes, undrained ❖ 1 (16 ounce) can kidney beans, rinsed and drained ❖ 1 (15 ounce) can black beans, rinsed and drained ❖ 1 (15 ounce) can pinto beans, rinsed and drained ❖ 1 (8 ounce) jar picante sauce ❖ 1 (8 ounce) can tomato sauce 1/2 cup water ❖ 1 (2.25 ounce) can sliced ripe olives, drained ❖ 1 teaspoon beef bouillon granules ❖ 1 teaspoon dried thyme ❖ 1 teaspoon salt ❖ 1/4 teaspoon pepper Shredded Cheddar cheese	In a large saucepan, cook the ham, onion, green pepper and garlic in oil until tender. Stir in tomatoes, beans, picante sauce, tomato sauce and water if desired. Bring to a boil. Stir in olives, bouillon, thyme, salt and pepper. Reduce heat, simmer, uncovered, for 15-20 minutes. Garnish with cheese

Massachusetts Straub Chili

Ingredients	Directions
❖ 3 tablespoons vegetable oil ❖ 2 large onions, chopped ❖ 1 green bell pepper, chopped ❖ 4 cloves garlic, minced ❖ 1/2 pound lean ground beef ❖ 1/2 pound beef stew meat, diced into 1 inch pieces ❖ 1 (28 ounce) can crushed tomatoes ❖ 1 (14 ounce) can beef broth ❖ 1/2 pound dry kidney beans ❖ 2 1/2 tablespoons chili powder ❖ 1 teaspoon Italian seasoning ❖ 1 teaspoon salt ❖ 2 tablespoons brown sugar	Heat oil in a large stockpot over medium heat. Saute onions and bell pepper until tender. Add garlic, ground beef and stew meat and cook until the meat is no longer pink, about 10 minutes. Add the tomatoes, beef broth and kidney beans to the stockpot, cover and bring to a boil. Let the mixture boil for 4 to 5 minutes then stir in the chili powder, Italian seasoning, salt and brown sugar. Simmer uncovered for about 2 hours, or until the chili thickens and beans are tender.

Chili Cheese Dip II

Ingredients	Directions
❖ 1 (8 ounce) package cream cheese, softened ❖ 1 (15 ounce) can chili with beans ❖ 1 pinch chili powder ❖ 1/2 tablespoon white sugar ❖ 1 (16 ounce) package corn chips	Cover cream cheese with chili in 1-1/2 quart microwaveable casserole dish. Cover and microwave until the chili and cream cheese stir together easily and become hot and bubbly. Add chili powder and sugar to taste. Serve hot with chips.

Insanely Easy Vegetarian Chili

Ingredients	Directions
<ul><li>1 tablespoon vegetable oil</li><li>1 cup chopped onions</li><li>3/4 cup chopped carrots</li><li>3 cloves garlic, minced</li><li>1 cup chopped green bell pepper</li><li>1 cup chopped red bell pepper3/4 cup chopped celery</li><li>1 tablespoon chili powder</li><li>1 1/2 cups chopped fresh mushrooms</li><li>1 (28 ounce) can whole peeled tomatoes with liquid, chopped</li><li>1 (19 ounce) can kidney beans with liquid</li><li>1 (11 ounce) can whole kernel corn, undrained</li><li>1 tablespoon ground cumin</li><li>1 1/2 teaspoons dried oregano</li><li>1 1/2 teaspoons dried basil</li></ul>	Heat oil in a large saucepan over medium heat. Saute onions, carrots, and garlic until tender. Stir in green pepper, red pepper, celery, and chili powder. Cook until vegetables are tender, about 6 minutes.Stir in mushrooms, and cook 4 minutes. Stir in tomatoes, kidney beans, and corn. Season with cumin, oregano, and basil. Bring to a boil, and reduce heat to medium. Cover, and simmer for 20 minutes, stirring occasionally

Chili con Carne III

Ingredients	Directions
<ul><li>large onion, finely chopped</li><li>1 clove garlic, peeled and crushed</li><li>2 teaspoons tomato paste</li><li>2 tablespoons butter, cut into pieces</li><li>2 tablespoons all-purpose flour</li><li>1 teaspoon dried oregano, crushed</li><li>1/2 teaspoon ground cumin</li><li>1 1/2 teaspoons chili powder</li><li>1 (14.5 ounce) can whole peeled tomatoes with liquid, chopped</li><li>1 pound lean ground beef</li><li>1 (15.25 ounce) can kidney beans,</li></ul>	In a large skillet over medium heat, combine onion, garlic, and tomato paste. Cover and cook for 5 minutes. Stir in butter until melted. Stir in flour, oregano, cumin, chili powder, tomatoes and beef. Cook uncovered for 8 minutes, stirring occasionally. Stir in the beans and cook for another 4 minutes, stirring occasionally. Salt and pepper to taste.

drained and rinsed ❖ salt to taste ground black pepper to taste	

Fifteen Minute Chicken Chili

Ingredients	Directions
❖ 1 tablespoon canola oil or extra virgin olive oil ❖ 10 ounces boneless, skinless chicken breast, cut in bite-sized pieces ❖ 1 1/2 tablespoons chili powder ❖ 1 1/2 tablespoons cumin ❖ 2 (14.5 ounce) cans no-salt-added diced tomatoes ❖ 1 (15 ounce) can no-salt-added black or red beans ❖ 1 (4.5 ounce) can minced green chilies ❖ 1 cup yellow whole-kernel corn, frozen or canned ❖ Salt and cayenne pepper, to taste	In a medium saucepan, saute chicken in oil over medium high heat for 3 minutes or until white. Stir in chili powder and cumin to coat chicken. Saute 3-4 minutes. Add remaining ingredients; heat through.

Chicken Chili I

Ingredients	Directions
❖ 1 (16 ounce) package dried navy beans ❖ 4 (14.5 ounce) cans chicken broth ❖ 1 onion, chopped ❖ 2 cloves garlic, minced ❖ 1 teaspoon ground black pepper ❖ 1 tablespoon dried oregano ❖ 1 tablespoon ground cumin 1/2 teaspoon ground cloves ❖ 5 cups chopped, cooked chicken meat ❖ 2 (4 ounce) cans diced green chile peppers ❖ 1 cup water ❖ 1 teaspoon salt ❖ 1 jalapeno pepper, seeded and minced	Sort and wash beans. Place beans, broth, onion, garlic, black pepper, oregano, cumin, and ground cloves in a Dutch oven. Bring to a boil. Cover, reduce heat, and simmer for 2 hours. Stir in chicken, chilies, water, salt, and jalapeno. Bring to a boil. Cover, reduce heat, and simmer for 1 hour; stirring often.

Quick Chili I

Ingredients	Directions
❖ 2 pounds ground beef ❖ 1 onion, finely diced ❖ 3 cloves garlic, minced ❖ 1 (14.5 ounce) can diced tomatoes ❖ 2 (14.5 ounce) cans Italian-style diced tomatoes ❖ 1 (8 ounce) can tomato sauce ❖ 1 cup water ❖ 1 (15 ounce) can kidney beans ❖ 1 (15 ounce) can pinto beans ❖ 2 tablespoons chili powder ❖ 1 tablespoon ground cumin ❖ 2 tablespoons white sugar ❖ 1 tablespoon salt ❖ 1 teaspoon ground black pepper ❖ 1 tablespoon hot pepper sauce	In a large stock pot lightly brown ground beef, and drain if needed. Add onion and garlic and cook until onion is translucent. Add tomatoes, diced tomatoes with chili peppers, tomato sauce, water, kidney beans, pinto beans, chili powder, cumin, sugar, salt, pepper and hot sauce. Simmer for 30 minutes and then serve.

Smokin' Scovilles Turkey Chili

Ingredients	Directions
❖ 2 tablespoons olive oil ❖ 1 onion, chopped ❖ 5 cloves garlic, minced ❖ 2 small green bell peppers, seeded and chopped ❖ 1 habanero pepper, seeded and chopped ❖ 2 pounds lean ground turkey ❖ 2 tablespoons chili powder ❖ 2 teaspoons red pepper flakes ❖ 1 tablespoon paprika ❖ 1 tablespoon ground cumin ❖ 2 teaspoons dried oregano ❖ 1 teaspoon ground black pepper ❖ 1 (1 ounce) envelope instant hot chocolate mix ❖ 2 teaspoons seasoned salt ❖ 1 tablespoon Worcestershire sauce ❖ 1 teaspoon liquid smoke flavoring ❖ 2 (14.5 ounce) cans diced tomatoes with green chile peppers, drained ❖ 1 (8 ounce) can tomato sauce ❖ 1 (15 ounce) can kidney beans, drained ❖ 1/2 cup cheap beer ❖ 1/2 cup canned whole kernel corn ❖ 1 tablespoon hot pepper sauce	Heat the olive oil in a large saucepan over medium heat. Add the onion, garlic, green peppers and habanero pepper; cook and stir until the onion is transparent. Push these to one side of the pot, and crumble in the ground turkey. Cover, and cook for about 5 minutes, stirring occasionally, or until the meat is no longer pink. Stir everything together so the garlic doesn't burn. Season with chili powder, red pepper flakes, paprika, cumin, oregano, pepper, hot cocoa mix and seasoned salt. Stir in Worcestershire sauce, liquid smoke, diced tomatoes with green chilies, tomato sauce and kidney beans. Crack open a beer, and pour in about 1/3. Drink or discard the rest. Partially cover the pan, and simmer over medium heat for about 50 minutes, stirring occasionally. Mix in the corn and hot pepper sauce, and simmer for about 10 more minutes. Remove from the heat and allow to cool for a few minutes before serving.

Best Ever Chuck Wagon Chili

Ingredients	Directions
<ul><li>2 pounds ground beef</li><li>1 teaspoon butter</li><li>2 large white onions, chopped</li><li>2 green bell peppers, seeded and chopped</li><li>1 habanero pepper, chopped</li><li>3 (15 ounce) cans kidney beans, drained</li><li>3 (15 ounce) cans tomato sauce</li><li>1 tablespoon chili powder</li><li>2 teaspoons salt</li><li>1/2 teaspoon garlic salt</li><li>1 drop super-hot hot pepper sauce</li></ul>	In a large pot, cook the ground beef over medium heat until evenly browned. Drain off grease, and set aside. Melt butter in a skillet over medium heat. Saute the onions, green pepper and habanero pepper until onions are translucent. Remove from heat. Transfer the onion mixture to the pot with the ground beef, and set the heat to medium. Add the kidney beans and tomato sauce to the beef mixture, and season with chili powder, salt, garlic salt and hot pepper sauce. Bring to a simmer, and adjust seasonings to taste if necessary. Cover, reduce heat to low, and simmer for 1 hour, stirring occasionally.

Nina's Texas Chili

Ingredients	Directions
<ul><li>2 teaspoons cooking oil</li><li>3 pounds beef top sirloin, thinly sliced</li><li>2 pounds sweet Italian sausage, casings removed</li><li>1 onion, chopped</li><li>1 green bell pepper, chopped</li><li>1 red bell pepper, chopped</li><li>1 yellow bell pepper, chopped</li><li>2 cloves garlic, minced</li><li>20 ounces diced tomatoes</li><li>3 (8 ounce) cans tomato sauce</li><li>2 teaspoons chicken bouillon granules</li><li>1/2 cup honey</li><li>1 (15 ounce) can kidney beans,</li></ul>	Heat the oil in a large pot over medium heat; cook the steak, sausage, onion, green pepper, red, pepper, yellow pepper, and garlic in the pot until the onions and peppers are soft, about 5 minutes. Add the diced tomatoes, tomato sauce, chicken bouillon, honey, and kidney beans; bring to a boil. One at a time, stir in the cayenne pepper, chili powder, oregano, black pepper, salt, and sugar. Sprinkle the Cheddar cheese into the chili in small batches and stir to melt. Reduce heat to low and slow cook about 2 hours. Thicken by stirring the masa through the chili, and simmering for 10 minutes.

rinsed and drained
- ❖ 2 tablespoons cayenne pepper
- ❖ 6 tablespoons chili powder
- ❖ 3 tablespoons dried oregano
- ❖ 1 teaspoon ground black pepper
- ❖ 2 teaspoons salt
- ❖ 1/3 cup white sugar
- ❖ 1 cup shredded Cheddar cheese
- ❖ 1/4 cup masa (corn flour)

It's Chili by George!!

Ingredients	Directions
<ul><li>❖ 2 pounds lean ground beef</li><li>❖ 1 (46 fluid ounce) can tomato juice</li><li>❖ 1 (29 ounce) can tomato sauce</li><li>❖ 1 (15 ounce) can kidney beans, drained and rinsed</li><li>❖ 1 (15 ounce) can pinto beans, drained and rinsed</li><li>❖ 1 1/2 cups chopped onion</li><li>❖ 1/4 cup chopped green bell pepper</li><li>❖ 1/8 teaspoon ground cayenne pepper</li><li>❖ 1/2 teaspoon white sugar</li><li>❖ 1/2 teaspoon dried oregano</li><li>❖ 1/2 teaspoon ground black pepper</li><li>❖ 1 teaspoon salt</li><li>❖ 1 1/2 teaspoons ground cumin 1/4 cup chili powder</li></ul>	Place ground beef in a large, deep skillet. Cook over medium-high heat until evenly brown. Drain, and crumble. In a large pot over high heat combine the ground beef, tomato juice, tomato sauce, kidney beans, pinto beans, onions, bell pepper, cayenne pepper, sugar, oregano, ground black pepper, salt, cumin and chili powder. Bring to a boil, then reduce heat to low. Simmer for 1 1/2 hours. (Note: If using a slow cooker, set on low, add ingredients, and cook for 8 to 10 hours.)

Chili Colorado

Ingredients	Directions
❖ 3 tablespoons all-purpose flour ❖ 1 1/2 pounds boneless pork, cut into 1 inch cubes ❖ 1 tablespoon bacon drippings, or vegetable oil ❖ 1 tablespoon vegetable oil ❖ 1 tablespoon all-purpose flour 1/4 cup chopped onion ❖ 1 (4 ounce) can tomato sauce ❖ 2 tablespoons chili powder ❖ 1 teaspoon cumin ❖ 1/2 teaspoon garlic powder salt and black pepper to taste ❖ 3 cups water	Place 3 tablespoons flour in a plastic bag. Add pork and shake to lightly coat with flour. Set aside. Heat bacon drippings and vegetable oil in a Dutch oven over medium high heat. Add pork and cook until meat is evenly browned, about 5 to 8 minutes. Stir in 1 tablespoon flour, and cook 3 minutes. Stir in the onion, tomato sauce, chile powder, cumin, garlic powder, salt, pepper, and water. Bring to a boil, then reduce heat to medium low and simmer until pork is just falling apart, about 1-1/2 to 2 hours.

Jim Kaczmarek's Chili

Ingredients	Directions
❖ 3 pounds beef chuck ❖ 2 1/2 cups chopped onions ❖ 5 cloves garlic, minced ❖ 2 (14.5 ounce) cans stewed tomatoes ❖ 1 (15 ounce) can tomato sauce ❖ 1 (12 fluid ounce) can or bottle beer ❖ 5 tablespoons chili powder ❖ 1 tablespoon dried oregano ❖ 1 tablespoon paprika ❖ 2 tablespoons ground cumin ❖ 1 tablespoon brown sugar ❖ 4 tablespoons beef bouillon granules ❖ 2 bay leaves ❖ 1 tablespoon salt ❖ 1 teaspoon ground black pepper	Place meat in freezer until slightly frozen. Cut into 1/4 to 1/2 inch cubes. In a large skillet over medium heat, brown meat until it turns gray. Stir in onions and garlic. Cook until onions are tender, about 5 to 10 minutes. Cut up canned tomatoes, reserving juice; combine in a 6 quart cooking pot with tomato sauce, beer, chili powder, oregano, paprika, cumin, brown sugar, beef base, bay leaves, salt, and pepper. Bring to a slow boil over high heat. Add meat mixture, and reduce heat to low. Simmer, uncovered, for 2 to 3 hours. Mix in pinto beans. Simmer for 1/2 hour

❖ 2 (15 ounce) cans pinto beans, drained	longer. Taste, and adjust seasonings if desired.

Skyline Chili I

Ingredients	Directions
❖ 2 1/2 pounds lean ground beef ❖ 1 (15 ounce) can tomato sauce ❖ 1 1/3 (6 ounce) cans tomato paste ❖ 5 tablespoons chili powder ❖ 2 teaspoons ground cinnamon ❖ 1 teaspoon ground allspice ❖ 1 1/4 teaspoons salt ❖ 1 tablespoon distilled white vinegar ❖ 1 teaspoon ground black pepper ❖ 1/4 teaspoon garlic powder ❖ 1 teaspoon onion salt ❖ 2 teaspoons steak sauce ❖ 1 quart water	Brown the beef lightly. Place all the ingredients in a crock pot and mix together well. Cook for 12 hours or more on low.

Darn Good Chili

Ingredients	Directions
❖ 1 pound lean ground beef ❖ 1 cup chopped onion ❖ 1/2 red bell pepper, chopped ❖ 3 tablespoons chili powder ❖ 2 teaspoons minced garlic ❖ 1 bay leaf ❖ 1 (14.5 ounce) can peeled and diced tomatoes ❖ 1 (15 ounce) can kidney beans, drained ❖ 1 cup spaghetti sauce ❖ 1 cup salsa ❖ 1/4 cup taco sauce	In a large saucepan or stockpot, cook ground beef, onion and red pepper until beef is browned. Drain off excess fat. Stir in the chili powder, garlic, bay leaf, diced tomatoes, spaghetti sauce, salsa and taco sauce. Lower heat and simmer for 1 ½ hours, stirring occasionally. Stir in beans just before serving and heat through.

Baked Snapper with Chilies, Ginger and Basil

Ingredients	Directions
❖ 1 (1 1/2 pound) whole red snapper, cleaned and scaled ❖ 1/2 cup fresh basil leaves ❖ 2 tablespoons peanut oil ❖ 2 tablespoons fish sauce ❖ 2 cloves garlic, minced ❖ 1 teaspoon minced fresh ginger ❖ 2 red chile peppers, sliced diagonally ❖ 1 yellow bell pepper, seeded and diced ❖ 1 tablespoon brown sugar ❖ 1 tablespoon rice vinegar ❖ 2 tablespoons water ❖ 2 tomatoes, seeded and sliced ❖ 5 leaves basil	Preheat oven to 375 degrees F (190 degrees C). Line a roasting pan with aluminum foil. Stuff the cavity of the snapper with 1/2 cup basil leaves and set aside. Heat the peanut oil in a large skillet over high heat until it begins to smoke. Place the snapper in the skillet, and quickly brown on both sides, about 1 minute total. Place the fish into the roasting pan, and sprinkle with fish sauce. Reserve the peanut oil in the skillet. Bake fish in preheated oven until the flesh flakes easily with a fork, 25 to 30 minutes. Meanwhile, heat the remaining peanut oil over medium heat. Stir in the garlic, ginger, chile peppers, and yellow pepper and cook until the peppers have softened, about 5 minutes. Stir in the sugar, rice vinegar, water, and tomatoes. Bring to a simmer over medium-high heat until thickened to desired consistency. Pour the sauce over the snapper, and garnish with the remaining basil leaves to serve.

Stove Top Tofu Chili

Ingredients	Directions
❖ 1/2 (12 ounce) package extra firm tofu ❖ 1 teaspoon chili powder ❖ 1 clove garlic, minced ❖ 2 tablespoons vegetable oil ❖ 1/2 cup onion, chopped ❖ 2 stalks celery, chopped ❖ 1/2 cup whole kernel corn, undrained ❖ 1 (15.25 ounce) can kidney beans, undrained ❖ 1 (14.5 ounce) can stewed tomatoes, undrained ❖ 1 quart water	In a medium bowl, crumble the tofu and toss with the chili powder and garlic. Heat the oil in a large saucepan over medium heat, and saute the onion and celery until tender. Stir in the tofu mixture. Continue cooking about 5 minutes over low heat. Mix in the corn, kidney beans, and stewed tomatoes. Add water and bring to a boil. Reduce heat to low and simmer about 50 minutes.

White Chili II

Ingredients	Directions
❖ 2 tablespoons olive oil ❖ 2 onions, chopped ❖ 4 cloves garlic, minced ❖ 4 cooked, boneless chicken breast half, chopped ❖ 3 (14.5 ounce) cans chicken broth ❖ 2 (4 ounce) cans canned green chile peppers, chopped ❖ 2 teaspoons ground cumin ❖ 2 teaspoons dried oregano ❖ 1 1/2 teaspoons cayenne pepper ❖ 5 (14.5 ounce) cans great Northern beans, undrained ❖ 1 cup shredded Monterey Jack cheese	Heat the oil in a large pot over medium heat. Add the onions and garlic and saute for 10 minutes, or until onions are tender. Add the chicken, chicken broth, green chile peppers, cumin, oregano and cayenne pepper and bring to a boil. Reduce heat to low and add the beans. Simmer for 20 to 30 minutes, or until heated thoroughly. Pour into individual bowls and top with the cheese.

Cheddar Chili Braid

Ingredients	Directions
❖ 1 (16 ounce) package hot roll mix ❖ 1 cup warm water (120 to 130 degrees F) ❖ 2 eggs ❖ 2 cups shredded Cheddar cheese ❖ 2 tablespoons canned chopped green chiles, drained ❖ 2 tablespoons grated Parmesan cheese	In a bowl, combine contents of roll mix and yeast packet; stir in water, one egg, cheddar cheese and chilies. Turn onto a floured surface; knead dough until smooth and elastic, about 5 minutes. Cover and let rest for 5 minutes. Divide into thirds. Shape each into a 14-in. rope. Place ropes on a greased baking sheet and braid; pinch ends to seal and tuck under. Cover and let rise in a warm place until doubled, about 30 minutes. Beat remaining egg; brush over dough. Sprinkle with Parmesan cheese. Bake at 375 degrees F for 30 minutes or until golden brown. Remove from pan to a wire rack

Texas Deer Chili

Ingredients	Directions
❖ 2 tablespoons vegetable oil ❖ 2 1/2 pounds venison, cut into cubes ❖ 1 large onion, chopped ❖ 1 clove garlic, minced ❖ 1 (4 ounce) can diced green chile peppers ❖ 2 (15 ounce) cans kidney beans, drained and rinsed ❖ 2 (10.5 ounce) cans beef broth ❖ 2 teaspoons dried oregano ❖ 2 teaspoons ground cumin ❖ 1/2 teaspoon salt ❖ 1 1/2 teaspoons paprika	In a large skillet over medium heat, cook venison, onion and garlic in oil until meat is browned. Transfer to a slow cooker and stir together with chiles, beans, broth oregano, cumin, salt and paprika. Cook on medium 4 to 5 hours.

White Chicken Chili

Ingredients	Directions
❖ 1 medium yellow onion, chopped ❖ 6 cups water ❖ 1 teaspoon lemon pepper ❖ 2 teaspoons ground cumin ❖ 1 (15 ounce) can hominy, drained ❖ 1 (15 ounce) can Great Northern beans, drained and rinsed ❖ 1 (7 ounce) can white corn ❖ 1 tablespoon light olive oil ❖ 2 (10 ounce) cans HORMEL® Premium Chunk Breast of Chicken ❖ 6 HERB-OX® Chicken Flavored Bouillon Cubes ❖ 1 (4.25 ounce) can CHI-CHI'S® Diced Green Chilies, drained	In large saucepan or Dutch oven, heat oil over medium-high heat. Add onion. Cook 4 to 5 minutes or until softened. Add water, chicken, bouillon, cumin and lemon pepper. Bring to a boil; reduce heat to medium-low. Cover. Simmer 5 minutes. Add hominy, beans, corn and chiles to saucepan. Cook 10 to 12 minutes or until hot and flavors are blended. Top with crushed tortilla chips and shredded cheese, if desired.

Mr. Bill's New Mexico Buffalo Chili

Ingredients	Directions
❖ 1 teaspoon unsweetened cocoa powder ❖ 1 teaspoon dried Mexican oregano ❖ 1 teaspoon dried basil ❖ 1 teaspoon dried marjoram ❖ 2 teaspoons ground cumin ❖ 1 tablespoon hot chili powder ❖ 1 teaspoon garlic powder ❖ 2 teaspoons hickory smoked salt ❖ 1 teaspoon ground black pepper ❖ 2 teaspoons cayenne pepper ❖ 2 pounds buffalo stew meat, cubed ❖ 2 pounds chorizo sausage, chopped ❖ 2 pounds pork stew meat, cubed	Whisk together the cocoa powder, Mexican oregano, basil, marjoram, cumin, hot chili powder, garlic powder, hickory salt, black pepper, and cayenne pepper. Combine the seasoning mix with the buffalo meat, chorizo, and pork; cover and refrigerate overnight. Heat a heavy skillet over medium heat, and fry the bacon until crisp. Remove the bacon with a slotted spoon to a large, heavy pot. In the same skillet, cook and stir the onion, habanero peppers, jalapeno peppers, garlic, and New Mexico chile powder in the bacon grease until onions are translucent; add the onion mixture to the pot. In the same skillet, fry the seasoned meat

- ❖ 2 slices hickory-smoked bacon, diced
- ❖ 3 sweet onions, coarsely chopped
- ❖ 2 habanero peppers, seeded and chopped
- ❖ 4 jalapeno peppers, seeded and chopped
- ❖ 7 cloves garlic, minced
- ❖ 2 teaspoons New Mexico chile powder
- ❖ 1 tablespoon lard, or more as needed
- ❖ 3 (10 ounce) cans diced tomatoes with green chile peppers (such as RO*TELB®), undrained
- ❖ 2 (7.75 ounce) cans salsa (such as El PatoB® Salsa de Chile Fresco)
- ❖ 1 (6 ounce) can tomato paste
- ❖ 1 (16 ounce) jar picante sauce (such as PaceB® Picante Sauce)
- ❖ 2 (4 ounce) cans diced green

in small batches until well browned, adding lard as needed; remove the meats to the pot. Stir the diced tomatoes with green chiles, salsa, tomato paste, picante sauce, diced green chiles, and dark beer into the pot. Simmer until the meat is easily pierced with a fork, 2 to 3 hours. If the chili seems too dry, add dark beer as needed.

Chili con Carne I

Ingredients	Directions
❖ 6 pounds dried pinto beans ❖ 3/8 cup salt ❖ 20 pounds lean ground beef ❖ 1 pound chopped onions ❖ 4 cloves garlic, minced ❖ 6 quarts canned peeled and diced tomatoes ❖ 2 quarts tomato paste ❖ 1 1/3 cups chili powder ❖ 3 tablespoons ground cumin ❖ 1 1/2 teaspoons ground black pepper	Wash and sort pinto beans. Bring 3 gallons of water to boil in a 6 gallon pot. Pour in beans, return to a boil and cook 2 minutes. Remove from heat and let stand 1 hour. Stir in salt and simmer until tender, 90 minutes. Drain and set aside. Brown beef with onions and garlic over medium high heat in same pot or enormous skillet. Combine meat mixture, tomatoes, tomato paste, chili powder, cumin, pepper and cooked beans in 6 gallon pot; stir; cover and simmer 1 hour.

White Bean Chicken Chili

Ingredients	Directions
❖ 2 tablespoons vegetable oil ❖ 1 onion, chopped ❖ 2 cloves garlic, minced ❖ 1 (14.5 ounce) can chicken broth ❖ 1 (18.75 ounce) can tomatillos, drained and chopped ❖ 1 (16 ounce) can diced tomatoes ❖ 1 (7 ounce) can diced green chiles ❖ 1/2 teaspoon dried oregano ❖ 1/2 teaspoon ground coriander seed ❖ 1/4 teaspoon ground cumin ❖ 2 ears fresh corn ❖ 1 pound diced, cooked chicken meat ❖ 1 (15 ounce) can white beans ❖ 1 pinch salt and black pepper to taste	Heat oil, and cook onion and garlic until soft. Stir in broth, tomatillos, tomatoes, chilies, and spices. Bring to a boil, then simmer for 10 minutes. Add corn, chicken, and beans; simmer 5 minutes. Season with salt and pepper to taste.

Chuck's Come On Ice Cream (or Night of the Red

Ingredients	Directions
❖ MEAT SEASONING ❖ 2 teaspoons ground sage ❖ 1 teaspoon dried thyme ❖ 1 teaspoon dried basil leaves ❖ 1 teaspoon dried marjoram ❖ 2 teaspoons ground cumin ❖ 1 tablespoon chili powder ❖ 1 teaspoon garlic powder ❖ 2 teaspoons salt ❖ 1 teaspoon ground black pepper ❖ 2 teaspoons cayenne pepper CHILI ❖ 3 pounds beef sirloin ❖ 3 pounds pork sirloin	To Marinate: The day before preparing the chili, in a large bowl mix together the sage, thyme, basil, marjoram, cumin, chili powder, garlic powder, salt, black pepper and cayenne pepper. Cut beef and pork into 1/2 inch cubes and add to bowl. Mix meat and seasoning together, cover bowl and refrigerate overnight. To Make Chili: Begin to heat tomatoes, tomato sauce, salsa and 2 teaspoons chili powder in a large pot over medium low heat. Meanwhile, heat bacon grease in a large skillet over medium heat. Add

- ❖ 2 (14.5 ounce) cans whole peeled tomatoes, chopped
- ❖ 2 (15 ounce) cans tomato sauce
- ❖ 1 (16 ounce) jar salsa
- ❖ 2 teaspoons chili powder
- ❖ 1 tablespoon bacon grease fresh jalapeno peppers, seeded and chopped
- ❖ 3 onions, chopped
- ❖ 7 cloves garlic, crushed salt to taste
- ❖ 2 scoops ice cream, any flavor

jalapeno peppers and saute until soft, 1 to 2 minutes, then add them to large pot.

In same skillet fry beef and pork with onion and garlic, in small batches, about 15 to 20 minutes each. As each batch is done add to large pot.

When all ingredients are in the large pot, season with salt to taste. Bring to a boil. Cover, reduce heat to medium low and simmer for about 3 hours. After eating chili, eat ice cream and say "Come on, ice cream!"

Chili Dog Casserole I

Ingredients	Directions
❖ 8 hot dog buns ❖ 8 hot dogs ❖ 1 (15 ounce) can chili ❖ 1/4 cup chopped onion ❖ 1 tablespoon prepared mustard ❖ 2 cups shredded Cheddar cheese	Preheat oven to 350 degrees F (175 degrees C). Lightly grease a 9x13 inch baking dish. Tear up the hot dog buns and arrange the pieces in the bottom of the dish evenly. Slice the hot dogs into bite size pieces and layer the pieces over the buns. Pour the chili over the hot dogs, sprinkle with the chopped onion, and then spread some mustard over the chili and the onion. Top off with the cheese. Bake at 350 degrees F (175 degrees C) for 30 minutes.

Bob Evans® Favorite Chili Recipe

Ingredients	Directions
❖ 1 pound Bob Evans® Original Recipe or Zesty Hot Sausage Roll ❖ 3/4 cup diced onion ❖ 3 teaspoons chili powder ❖ 1 teaspoon ground cumin ❖ 3/4 teaspoon garlic powder ❖ 1 (15 ounce) can tomato sauce ❖ 1 (15 ounce) can light red kidney beans (including liquid) ❖ 3/4 cup water ❖ 1 (14.5 ounce) can diced tomatoes	In large saucepan over medium heat, crumble and cook sausage and onion until sausage is brown. Add chili powder, cumin and garlic and stir for 2 minutes. Add remaining ingredients and stir well. Bring to a boil, reduce heat to low and simmer for 20 minutes.

Wazzu Tailgate Chili

Ingredients	Directions
❖ 1 pound ground beef ❖ 1 pound ground pork ❖ 2 tablespoons olive oil ❖ 1 large onion, chopped, divided ❖ 1 green bell pepper, chopped ❖ 1 habanero peppers, seeded and minced ❖ 2 jalapeno pepper, seeded and minced ❖ 3 cloves garlic, minced ❖ 3 tablespoons chopped green onion ❖ 3 (15 ounce) cans chili beans ❖ 1 (14.5 ounce) can diced tomatoes ❖ 1 (6 ounce) can tomato paste ❖ 1 (8 ounce) can tomato sauce ❖ 1 (12 ounce) bottle lager-style beer ❖ 2 tablespoons cornmeal ❖ 1 cup water ❖ 1/4 cup chili powder ❖ 1 tablespoon ground cumin ❖ 1 teaspoon garlic powder ❖ 1/2 teaspoon cayenne pepper	Cook ground beef and pork in a large skillet over medium-high heat until the meat is crumbly, evenly browned, and no longer pink. Drain and discard any excess grease. Meanwhile, heat the olive oil in a large pot over medium heat. Stir in 3/4 of the onion and all of the green pepper, habanero pepper, jalapeno pepper, and garlic. Cook and stir until the onion has softened and turned translucent, about 5 minutes. Stir the drained meat into the onion mixture along with the green onion, chili beans, diced tomatoes, tomato paste, tomato sauce, beer, and water. Sprinkle with the cornmeal, then season with chili powder, cumin, garlic powder, cayenne pepper, salt, and black pepper. Bring to a simmer over medium heat, and then reduce heat to medium-low. Simmer at least 2 hours, stirring occasionally. Refrigerate overnight.

❖ 1 tablespoon salt ❖ 1 1/2 teaspoons ground black pepper ❖ 1 cup shredded Cheddar cheese	Reheat the chili over medium heat until it begins to simmer again. Top individual servings of chili with cheese and remaining chopped onion.

Chili Cheese Fries

Ingredients	Directions
❖ 1 (32 ounce) package frozen seasoned french fries ❖ 2 tablespoons cornstarch ❖ 2 tablespoons water ❖ 2 cups low-fat milk ❖ 1 tablespoon margarine ❖ 8 slices American cheese, cut into pieces ❖ 1 (15 ounce) can chili without beans (such as Hormel®)	Prepare french fries as directed on the package. Stir cornstarch and water in a small cup until cornstarch dissolves; set aside. Bring milk and margarine to a boil in a saucepan, stirring constantly. Reduce the heat and whisk the cornstarch mixture into the milk mixture, bring to a simmer over medium heat. Cook and stir until the mixture is thick and smooth. Add the cheese to the milk mixture and stir until the cheese has melted and is well combined. Prepare chili as directed on the can. Pour the cooked chili and the cheese sauce over the top of the cooked french fries.

Maverick Moose Chili

Ingredients	Directions
❖ 1 pound ground moose ❖ 1 (28 ounce) can diced tomatoes with green chile peppers ❖ 2 (15 ounce) cans chili beans, undrained ❖ 2 (14 ounce) cans kidney beans, rinsed and drained ❖ 2 (14.5 ounce) cans pinto beans,	Brown the ground moose in a large skillet over medium-high heat. Combine the moose, diced tomatoes, chili beans, kidney beans, pinto beans, olives, onion, and bell pepper in a slow cooker; stir in the chili seasoning. Set the slow cooker to Low; cook 8 to 12 hours.

rinsed and drained
- ❖ 2 (2.25 ounce) cans sliced black olives
- ❖ 1 white onion, chopped
- ❖ 1 green bell pepper, chopped
- ❖ 1 (1.25 ounce) package chili seasoning mix

Southwestern Three-Meat Chili

Ingredients	Directions
❖ 3 pounds ground beef ❖ 1 pound pork tenderloin, cut into 1/2 inch cubes ❖ 1 pound bulk Italian sausage ❖ 2 large onions, chopped ❖ 2 celery ribs, diced ❖ 1 medium green pepper, diced ❖ 3 garlic cloves, minced ❖ 2 (28 ounce) cans diced tomatoes, undrained ❖ 3 (15 ounce) cans pinto beans, drained and rinsed ❖ 1 (16 ounce) can kidney beans, rinsed and drained ❖ 2 (4 ounce) cans chopped green chilies ❖ 1 (8 ounce) can tomato sauce ❖ 1 cup beef broth ❖ 1 (6 ounce) can tomato paste ❖ 7 1/2 teaspoons chili powder ❖ 2 tablespoons ground cumin ❖ 2 tablespoons lemon juice ❖ 1 tablespoon all-purpose flour ❖ 1 tablespoon dried oregano ❖ 1 tablespoon brown sugar ❖ 1 1/2 teaspoons salt ❖ 1/2 teaspoon pepper ❖ 2 bay leaves	In a soup kettle or Dutch oven, cook the beef, pork and sausage over medium heat until no longer pink; drain. Add the onions, celery, green pepper and garlic; cook for 8-10 minutes or until vegetables are tender. Stir in the remaining ingredients. Bring to a boil. Reduce heat; simmer, uncovered for 1-1/2 hours. Discard bay leaves before serving.

Black Bean and Chickpea Chili

Ingredients	Directions
❖ 1 1/2 tablespoons olive oil ❖ 1 pound ground turkey (optional) ❖ 1 onion, chopped ❖ 2 green bell peppers, seeded and chopped ❖ 5 carrots, peeled and sliced into rounds ❖ 1 tablespoon chili powder ❖ 1 1/2 teaspoons ground cumin ❖ 1 teaspoon ground black pepper ❖ 2 (14.5 ounce) cans canned diced tomatoes with their juice ❖ 1 cup frozen corn ❖ 1 (15 ounce) can black beans, drained and rinsed ❖ 1 (15 ounce) can garbanzo beans, drained and rinsed ❖ 1 1/2 cups chicken broth	If using turkey, heat oil in a large saucepan over medium-high heat, and cook and stir the ground turkey for about 10 minutes, breaking it up with a spoon as it cooks, until the meat is no longer pink. Remove the turkey meat and set aside, leaving oil in the pan. Place the onion, green peppers, and carrots into the saucepan, and cook and stir for about 10 minutes, until the onion is translucent and the vegetables are tender. Stir in the chili powder, cumin, and black pepper, and pour in the diced tomatoes, frozen corn, black beans, garbanzo beans, and chicken broth. Bring the mixture to a boil. Place about 1 1/2 cups of the chili mixture into a food processor, and puree for about 1 minute until smooth. Pour the puree back into the rest of the chili to thicken. Add the cooked turkey meat, and bring the chili back to a simmer over medium-low heat.

Chili-Lime Chicken Kabobs

Ingredients	Directions
❖ 3 tablespoons olive oil ❖ 1 1/2 tablespoons red wine vinegar ❖ 1 lime, juiced ❖ 1 teaspoon chili powder ❖ 1/2 teaspoon paprika ❖ 1/2 teaspoon onion powder ❖ 1/2 teaspoon garlic powder cayenne pepper to taste ❖ salt and freshly ground black pepper to taste ❖ 1 pound skinless, boneless chicken breast halves - cut into 1 1/2 inch pieces ❖ skewers	In a small bowl, whisk together the olive oil, vinegar, and lime juice. Season with chili powder, paprika, onion powder, garlic powder, cayenne pepper, salt, and black pepper. Place the chicken in a shallow baking dish with the sauce, and stir to coat. Cover, and marinate in the refrigerator at least 1 hour. Preheat the grill for medium-high heat. Thread chicken onto skewers, and discard marinade. Lightly oil the grill grate. Grill skewers for 10 to 15 minutes, or until the chicken juices run clear.

Aush (Afghani Chili)

Ingredients	Directions
❖ 1 pound ground beef ❖ 1 onion, coarsely chopped ❖ 1 (28 ounce) can diced tomatoes, with juice ❖ 1 tablespoon minced garlic ❖ 1 teaspoon crushed red pepper flakes ❖ 1 1/2 tablespoons ground cumin ❖ 2 teaspoons chili powder ❖ 1 1/2 tablespoons dried mint ❖ 2 tablespoons garam masala ❖ 1 (15 ounce) can garbanzo beans (chickpeas), drained ❖ 1 (10 ounce) box frozen chopped spinach ❖ 1 (16 ounce) package fettuccine, broken in half ❖ 1 cup sour cream	Brown ground beef in a skillet over medium heat; remove with slotted spoon to a large pot; reserving drippings in the skillet. Cook and stir the onion in the reserved drippings until golden brown; remove with slotted spoon and add to beef in the pot. Stir the tomatoes with juice, garlic, red pepper, cumin, chili powder, mint, garam masala, garbanzo beans, and spinach into the beef mixture and place the pot over low heat; simmer 3 to 6 hours. Fill a large pot with lightly salted water and bring to a rolling boil over high heat. Once the water is boiling, stir in the fettuccini, and return to a boil. Cook the pasta uncovered, stirring occasionally,

until the pasta has cooked through, but is still firm to the bite, about 8 minutes. Drain well in a colander set in the sink. Stir into the chili along with the sour cream and serve hot.

Chili Chops

Ingredients	Directions
❖ 4 (1/2-inch thick) bone-in pork loin chops ❖ 4 slices onion, 1/4 inch thick ❖ 4 slices green pepper ❖ 1 (12 ounce) bottle chili sauce	Place the pork chops in a greased 9-in. square baking dish. Top with the onion, green pepper and chili sauce. Cover and bake at 350 degrees F for 20-30 minutes or until meat juices run clear.

Chili-Stuffed Peppers

Ingredients	Directions
❖ 6 medium green bell peppers ❖ 1 pound ground beef ❖ 1/2 cup chopped onion ❖ 1 (15 ounce) can chili beans, undrained ❖ 1 (10 ounce) can diced tomatoes and green chilies, undrained ❖ 1 teaspoon chili powder ❖ 1/2 teaspoon salt ❖ 1/4 teaspoon pepper ❖ 1/4 teaspoon cayenne pepper 3/4 cup shredded Cheddar cheese	Cut tops off peppers and remove seeds. Place peppers in a large kettle and cover with water. Bring to a boil; cook until crisp-tender, about 3 minutes. Drain and rinse in cold water, about 3 minutes. Drain and rinse in cold water; set aside. In a arge skillet, cook beef and onion over medium heat until meat is no longer pink; drain. Add beans, tomatoes, chili powder, salt if desired, pepper and cayenne. Bring to a boil. Reduce heat; cover and simmer for 5 minutes. Spoon meat mixture into peppers; place in an ungreased 3-qt. baking dish. Cover and bake at 350 degrees F for 20-25 minutes or until heated through. Sprinkle with cheese.

Chili-Cheese Spoon Bread

Ingredients	Directions
❖ 1/2 cup egg substitute 1 egg ❖ 1 (8.75 ounce) can whole kernel corn, drained ❖ 1 (8 ounce) can cream-style corn ❖ 1 cup reduced-fat sour cream ❖ 1 cup shredded reduced-fat Cheddar cheese ❖ 1 cup shredded reduced-fat Mexican cheese blend or part-skim mozzarella cheese ❖ 1 (4 ounce) can chopped green chilies, drained ❖ 1/2 cup cornmeal ❖ 2 tablespoons butter or stick	In a large bowl, beat egg substitute and egg. Add the remaining ingredients; mix well. Pour into a 9-in. square baking dish coated with nonstick cooking spray. Bake at 350 degrees F for 35-40 minutes or until a knife inserted near the center comes out clean. Serve warm.

margarine, melted ❖ 1/2 teaspoon salt ❖ 1/2 teaspoon Worcestershire sauce ❖ 1/8 teaspoon cayenne pepper	

Chili Corn Bread Wedges

Ingredients	Directions
❖ 1 (8.5 ounce) package corn bread/muffin mix ❖ 1 egg ❖ 1/3 cup milk ❖ 1 (4 ounce) can chopped green chilies ❖ 2 tablespoons sugar ❖ 3/4 cup frozen corn, thawed	Place corn bread mix in a large bowl. Combine the egg, milk, chilies and sugar; stir into mix just until moistened. Fold in corn. Pour into a greased 9-in. round baking pan. Bake at 400 degrees F for 20-25 minutes or until a toothpick inserted near the center comes out clean. Cool on a wire rack for 5 minutes. Cut into wedges; serve warm.

Speedy Chili Mac

Ingredients	Directions
❖ 2 cups uncooked elbow macaroni ❖ 1 1/2 teaspoons dried minced onion ❖ 1 (15 ounce) can chili without beans ❖ 1 (10.75 ounce) can condensed cream of mushroom soup, ❖ undiluted ❖ 1 cup shredded Cheddar cheese, divided	In a saucepan, cook macaroni in boiling water for 5 minutes. Stir in onion. Cook 1-2 minutes longer or until macaroni is tender; drain. In another saucepan, combine the chili and soup; heat through. Stir in macaroni and 3/4 cup of cheese. Transfer to a greased 11-in. x 7- in. x 2-in. baking dish. Cover and bake at 350 degrees F for 20 minutes. Uncover; sprinkle with remaining cheese. Bake 5-10 minutes longer or until cheese is melted.

Pressure Cooker Chili

Ingredients	Directions
❖ 1 pound ground beef ❖ 2 teaspoons olive oil ❖ 1 sweet onion, chopped ❖ 1 small green bell pepper, finely chopped ❖ 1 jalapeno pepper, seeded and finely chopped ❖ 2 cloves garlic, minced ❖ 2 (14.5 ounce) cans dark red kidney beans, drained and rinsed ❖ 2 (14.5 ounce) cans diced tomatoes, undrained ❖ 3 tablespoons tomato paste ❖ 1 tablespoon dark brown sugar ❖ 2 teaspoons unsweetened cocoa powder ❖ 1/4 teaspoon crushed red pepper flakes, or to taste ❖ 2 tablespoons chili powder ❖ 2 teaspoons ground cumin	Place the ground beef in the pressure cooker over medium high heat; cook until brown and crumbly, 8 to 10 minutes. Remove the ground beef, and drain off the excess fat. Return the open pressure cooker to the burner over medium heat, pour in the olive oil, and stir in the onion, green pepper, and jalapeno pepper. Cook and stir for 3 to 4 minutes, until the onion is translucent. Add the garlic, and cook and stir for about 30 more seconds. Return the meat to the pressure cooker; mix in the kidney beans, diced tomatoes, tomato paste, brown sugar, cocoa powder, red pepper flakes, chili powder, cumin, salt, and water. Lock the lid, bring the cooker up to pressure, reduce heat to maintain

❖ 1/2 teaspoon kosher salt, or to taste ❖ 2 cups water	pressure, and cook for 8 minutes. Remove cooker from the heat, and let the pressure reduce on its own, 5 to 10 minutes. When the pressure is fully released, remove the lid, stir the chili, and serve.

Coriander and Chili Almonds

Ingredients	Directions
❖ 1/2 tablespoon olive oil ❖ 1 1/2 cups blanched California Almonds ❖ 1 teaspoon coriander seeds, crushed ❖ 1 dried red chile pepper ❖ 2 pinches of sea salt	Add the olive oil and almonds to a hot saute pan. Saute the almonds until golden brown, shaking the pan regularly to color them evenly and accentuate their nutty flavor. Crumble in the coriander and chili to taste, and add the sea salt. Toss over and serve hot on a large plate.

Polish Chili

Ingredients	Directions
❖ 2 pounds ground beef ❖ 1 pound fully cooked Polish sausage or kielbasa, chopped ❖ 1 large onion, chopped ❖ 3 cloves garlic, minced ❖ 4 Anaheim chilies, stemmed, seeded, and chopped ❖ 3 yellow wax peppers, seeded and chopped ❖ 3 jalapeno peppers, seeded and chopped ❖ 4 medium tomatoes, chopped ❖ 4 tomatillos, husked and chopped ❖ 1/2 cup distilled white vinegar ❖ 1/4 cup tomato sauce ❖ 1 (4 ounce) jar chopped pimentos, drained ❖ 1 (15 ounce) can pinto beans, rinsed and drained ❖ 1 (15 ounce) can kidney beans, rinsed and drained	Place the ground beef into a large pot over medium-high heat. Cook, stirring to crumble, until beef is no longer pink. Drain off excess grease, leaving just enough to coat the bottom of the pot. Add the polish sausage, onion and garlic to the pot; cook and stir until onion is tender. Mix in the Anaheim, yellow and jalapeno peppers, tomatoes and tomatillos. Simmer over medium heat for about 20 minutes. Pour in the vinegar, tomato sauce and pimentos and then mix in the pinto beans and kidney beans; cover and simmer over medium heat for 30 minutes.

Slow-Cooked White Chili

Ingredients	Directions
❖ 3/4 pound skinless, boneless chicken breast halves - cubed ❖ 1 medium onion, chopped ❖ 1 garlic clove, minced ❖ 1 tablespoon vegetable oil ❖ 1 1/2 cups water ❖ 1 (15 ounce) can white kidney or cannelini beans, rinsed and ❖ drained ❖ 1 (15 ounce) can garbanzo beans, rinsed and drained ❖ 1 (11 ounce) can whole kernel	In a large skillet, saute chicken, onion and garlic in oil until onion is tender. Transfer to a slow cooker. Stir in the remaining ingredients. Cover and cook on low for 7-8 hours or until chicken juices run clear and flavors are blended.

corn, drained
- ❖ 1 (4 ounce) can chopped green chilies
- ❖ 1 teaspoon chicken bouillon granules
- ❖ 1 teaspoon ground cumin

White Chili with Ground Turkey

Ingredients	Directions
<ul><li>❖ 1 onion, chopped</li><li>❖ 3 cloves garlic, minced</li><li>❖ 1 1/2 pounds ground turkey</li><li>❖ 2 (4 ounce) cans canned green chile peppers, chopped</li><li>❖ 1 tablespoon ground cumin</li><li>❖ 1 tablespoon dried oregano</li><li>❖ 1 teaspoon ground cinnamon ground cayenne pepper to taste ground white pepper to taste</li><li>❖ 3 (15 ounce) cans cannellini beans</li><li>❖ 5 cups chicken broth</li><li>❖ 2 cups shredded Monterey Jack cheese</li></ul>	In a large pot over medium heat, combine the onion, garlic and ground turkey and saute for 10 minutes, or until turkey is well browned. Add the chile peppers, cumin, oregano, cinnamon, cayenne pepper to taste and white pepper to taste and saute for 5 more minutes. Add two cans of the beans and the chicken broth to the pot. Take the third can of beans and puree them in a blender or food processor. Add this to the pot along with the cheese. Stir well and simmer for 10 minutes, allowing the cheese to melt.

Cincinnati Skyline Chili

Ingredients	Directions
❖ 2 pounds lean ground beef ❖ 1 onion, chopped ❖ 2 (8 ounce) cans tomato sauce ❖ 1 clove garlic, crushed ❖ 1 dash Worcestershire sauce ❖ 1 pinch ground cinnamon ❖ 1 teaspoon distilled white vinegar ❖ 3 tablespoons chili powder ❖ 1 pinch cayenne pepper salt and pepper to taste ❖ 1 pound uncooked spaghetti ❖ 1 cup shredded Cheddar cheese ❖ 1 cup kidney beans ❖ 1/2 cup olives ❖ 1/4 cup chopped onion	Brown beef and onion in a large skillet over medium high heat. Place browned mixture in a large pot and stir in the tomato sauce, garlic, Worcestershire sauce, cinnamon, vinegar, chili powder, cayenne pepper, salt and pepper. Simmer, uncovered, over low heat for 1 1/2 hours. When meat mixture has about 20 minutes cooking time left, bring a large pot of lightly salted water to a boil. Add pasta and cook for 8 to 10 minutes or until al dente; drain and set aside. Serve meat mixture over cooked spaghetti topped with cheese, beans, olives and chopped onion.

Sausage Corn Chili

Ingredients	Directions
❖ 1 pound bulk Italian sausage ❖ 1 tablespoon dried minced onion ❖ 1 (16 ounce) can kidney beans, rinsed and drained ❖ 1 (15.25 ounce) can whole kernel corn, drained ❖ 1 (15 ounce) can tomato sauce ❖ 2/3 cup picante sauce ❖ 1/3 cup water ❖ 1 teaspoon chili powder	In a large saucepan, cook sausage and onion over medium heat until meat is no longer pink; drain. Stir in the remaining ingredients. Simmer, uncovered, for 5-10 minutes or until heated through.

Rotisserie Chicken Chili With Hominy & Chiles

Ingredients	Directions
❖ 2 store-bought roast chickens, meat picked from bones and ❖ 2 quarts chicken broth ❖ 6 tablespoons vegetable oil ❖ 1/4 cup ground cumin ❖ 4 teaspoons dried oregano ❖ 1/2 teaspoon cayenne pepper ❖ 2 large onions, cut into medium dice ❖ 2 (4 ounce) jars diced mild green chiles ❖ 2 (20 ounce) cans hominy, or equal quantity of canned white beans, such as cannellini or great Northern ❖ 6 medium garlic cloves, minced ❖ 2 cups frozen corn, preferably shoepeg ❖ sour cream ❖ cilantro or scallions lime wedges ❖ green hot sauce	Bring skin and bones, chicken broth and 1 quart of water to boil over medium-high heat. Reduce heat to low and simmer about 30 minutes. Strain and discard skin and bones. Heat oil over medium-low heat in a soup kettle. Add cumin, oregano and cayenne and cook until spices are fragrant, about 1 minute. Add onion; increase heat to medium; saute until soft, 4 to 5 minutes. Stir in chicken and chiles. Add 4 cups hominy and all but 1 cup of the broth and bring to a simmer. Reduce heat to low and simmer, uncovered, stirring occasionally, 25 to 30 minutes. Process remaining 2 cups hominy and 1 cup broth until silky smooth; add to soup. Stir garlic and corn into soup. Simmer for a minute or so longer, then cover and let stand for 5 minutes. Ladle into bowls and top with sour cream, cilantro or scallions. Pass separately the lime wedges and green hot pepper sauce.

Smokin' Texas Chili

Ingredients	Directions
❖ 2 tablespoons olive oil ❖ 1 1/2 pounds boneless beef sirloin steak or top round steak, 3/4-inch thick, cut into 1/2-inch pieces ❖ 1 medium onion, chopped ❖ 2 cloves garlic, minced ❖ 3 cups Pace® Chunky Salsa, any variety ❖ 1/2 cup water ❖ 1 tablespoon chili powder ❖ 1 teaspoon ground cumin ❖ 1 (15 ounce) can red kidney beans, rinsed and drained ❖ 1/4 cup chopped fresh cilantro leaves ❖ Chili Toppings	Heat 1 tablespoon oil in a 6-quart saucepot over medium-high heat. Add the beef in 2 batches and cook until it's well browned, stirring often. Remove the beef from the saucepot. Add the remaining oil and heat over medium heat. Add the onion and cook until it's tender. Add the garlic and cook for 30 seconds. Add the salsa, water, chili powder and cumin. Heat to a boil. Return the beef to the saucepot. Stir in the beans. Reduce the heat to low. Cover and cook for 1 hour. Uncover and cook for 30 minutes or until the beef is fork-tender. Sprinkle with the cilantro and Chili Toppings, if desired.

Chili Barbecue Chops

Ingredients	Directions
❖ 1/2 cup Italian salad dressing ❖ 1/2 cup barbecue sauce ❖ 2 teaspoons chili powder ❖ 4 (3/4 inch) thick bone-in pork chops	In a bowl, combine the salad dressing, barbecue sauce and chili powder; mix well. Pour 1/2 cup marinade into a large resealable plastic bag; add the pork chops. Seal bag and turn to coat; refrigerate for at least 1 hour. Cover and refrigerate remaining marinade. Drain and discard marinade from pork. In a large skillet coated with nonstick cooking spray, brown chops on both sides over medium heat; drain. Add reserved marinade. Bring to a boil. Reduce heat; cover and simmer for 5-7 minutes or until a meat thermometer reaches 160 degrees F.

Penne with Chili, Chicken, and Prawns

Ingredients	Directions
❖ 1 (8 ounce) package uncooked penne pasta ❖ 2 skinless, boneless chicken breast halves - cubed ❖ 5 slices bacon ❖ 3 cloves garlic, chopped ❖ 1 (26 ounce) jar spicy red pepper pasta sauce ❖ 1/2 pound medium shrimp - peeled and deveined ❖ 1 fresh red chile pepper, finely chopped ❖ 1 cup grated Parmesan cheese	Bring a large pot of lightly salted water to a boil. Place penne pasta in the pot, cook for 8 to 10 minutes, until al dente, and drain. Place chicken, bacon, and garlic in a large skillet over medium heat, and cook 10 minutes, until bacon is evenly brown and chicken juices run clear. Drain grease. Mix pasta sauce into skillet. Continue cooking until sauce is heated through. Mix in shrimp. Cook 2 minutes, or until shrimp are opaque. Stir in chile pepper. Toss with cooked pasta and 1/2 the Parmesan cheese just before serving. Garnish with remaining Parmesan.

Easy Homemade Chili

Ingredients	Directions
❖ 1 pound ground beef ❖ 1 onion, chopped ❖ 1 (14.5 ounce) can stewed tomatoes ❖ 1 (15 ounce) can tomato sauce ❖ 1 (15 ounce) can kidney beans ❖ 1 1/2 cups water ❖ 1 pinch chili powder ❖ 1 pinch garlic powder salt and pepper to taste	In a large saucepan over medium heat, combine the beef and onion and saute until meat is browned and onion is tender. Add the stewed tomatoes with juice, tomato sauce, beans and water. Season with the chili powder, garlic powder, salt and ground black pepper to taste. Bring to a boil, reduce heat to low, cover and let simmer for 15 minutes.

Carol's Chicken Chili

Ingredients	Directions
❖ 1 tablespoon olive oil ❖ 6 skinless, boneless chicken breast halves - chopped ❖ 1 cup chopped onion ❖ 1 1/2 cups chicken broth ❖ 1 (4 ounce) can chopped green chile peppers ❖ 1 teaspoon garlic powder ❖ 1 teaspoon ground cumin ❖ 1/2 teaspoon dried oregano ❖ 1/2 teaspoon dried cilantro ❖ 1/8 teaspoon crushed red pepper ❖ 2 (19 ounce) cans cannellini beans, drained and rinsed ❖ 2 green onions, chopped ❖ 3/4 cup shredded Monterey Jack cheese	Heat oil in a large pot over medium high heat. Add chicken and onion and saute for 4 to 5 minutes. Stir in broth, chile peppers, garlic powder, cumin, oregano, cilantro and red pepper. Reduce heat to low and simmer for 15 minutes. Stir in beans and simmer for 10 minutes; top with green onion and cheese and serve.

Chili Cups

Ingredients	Directions
❖ 1 pound ground beef ❖ 1 medium green pepper, diced ❖ 1 medium onion, diced ❖ 3 garlic cloves, minced ❖ 1 (8 ounce) can tomato sauce ❖ 2 tablespoons water ❖ 1/2 teaspoon salt ❖ 1/2 teaspoon ground cumin ❖ 1/2 teaspoon dried oregano ❖ 1/4 teaspoon celery seed ❖ 1/4 teaspoon dill weed ❖ 1/8 teaspoon cayenne pepper ❖ 2 (1 pound) loaves sliced Italian bread ❖ grated Parmesan cheese	In a large skillet, brown beef, green pepper, onion and garlic; drain. Stir in tomato sauce, water and seasonings. Bring to a boil over medium heat. Reduce heat; cover and simmer for 30 minutes, stirring occasionally. Meanwhile, cut 2-1/2-in circles from bread slices using a biscuit cutter. Press the circles into greased miniature muffin cups. Bake at 400 degrees F for 5-6 minutes or until lightly toasted. Remove from tins and cool on wire racks. Fill each bread cup with about 1 tablespoon chili mixture; sprinkle with Parmesan cheese. Broil for 2-3 minutes or until cheese is golden brown.

Butternut Squash and Turkey Chili

Ingredients	Directions
❖ 2 tablespoons olive oil ❖ 1 onion, chopped ❖ 2 cloves garlic, minced ❖ 1 pound ground turkey breast ❖ 1 pound butternut squash - peeled, seeded and cut into 1-inch dice ❖ 1/2 cup chicken broth ❖ 1 (4.5 ounce) can chopped green chilies ❖ 2 (14.5 ounce) cans petite diced tomatoes ❖ 1 (15 ounce) can kidney beans with liquid ❖ 1 (15.5 ounce) can white hominy, drained ❖ 1 (8 ounce) can tomato sauce ❖ 1 tablespoon chili powder ❖ 1 tablespoon ground cumin ❖ 1 teaspoon garlic salt	Heat the olive oil in a large pot over medium heat. Stir in the onion and garlic; cook and stir for 3 minutes, then add the turkey, and stir until crumbly and no longer pink. Add the butternut squash, chicken broth, green chilies, tomatoes, kidney beans, hominy, and tomato sauce; season with chili powder, cumin, and garlic salt. Bring to a simmer, then reduce heat to medium-low, cover, and simmer until the squash is tender, about 20 minutes.

Chili Bean Nacho Skillet

Ingredients	Directions
❖ 1 pound ground beef 1/2 cup chopped onion ❖ 1 (15.5 ounce) can chili beans, undrained ❖ 1 (15 ounce) can tomato sauce ❖ 1 (11 ounce) can Mexicorn, drained ❖ 1 teaspoon sugar ❖ 1 teaspoon chili powder ❖ 1/2 teaspoon dried oregano ❖ 1/2 cup shredded Cheddar cheese ❖ Tortilla chips	In a large skillet, cook beef and onion over medium heat until meat is no longer pink; drain. Stir in the beans, tomato sauce, corn, sugar, chili powder and oregano. Bring to a boil. Reduce heat; simmer, uncovered, for 10 minutes. Sprinkle with cheese; remove from the heat. Cover; let stand for 5 minutes or until cheese is melted. Serve with tortilla chips if desired.

Kas' Chili

Ingredients	Directions
<ul><li>2 pounds ground beef</li><li>2 green bell peppers, chopped</li><li>2 onions, chopped</li><li>2 (15.25 ounce) cans kidney beans, rinsed and drained</li><li>1 (15 ounce) can black beans</li><li>1 (8 ounce) can tomato sauce</li><li>2 (14.5 ounce) cans diced tomatoes</li><li>1 tablespoon minced garlic</li><li>2 1/2 tablespoons chili powder</li><li>1 1/2 teaspoons paprika</li><li>1 tablespoon dried oregano</li><li>1 teaspoon dried rosemary</li><li>1 teaspoon ground coriander</li><li>1 teaspoon garlic powder</li><li>1 1/2 teaspoons salt</li><li>2 tablespoons ground cumin</li><li>1/4 cup chopped fresh cilantro</li><li>2 bay leaves</li></ul>	Place a large skillet over medium-high heat. Cook the ground beef in the hot skillet until completely browned, 7 to 10 minutes; drain. Combine the drained beef in a slow cooker with the bell peppers, onions, kidney beans, black beans, tomato sauce, and diced tomatoes. Cook on High for 30 minutes. Stir the garlic, chili powder, paprika, oregano, rosemary, coriander, garlic powder, salt, cumin, cilantro, and bay leaves into the beef mixture. Reduce heat to Low and cook another 6 1/2 hours.

Venison Tequila Chili

Ingredients	Directions
<ul><li>2 tablespoons vegetable oil</li><li>3 pounds ground venison</li><li>2 stalks celery, diced</li><li>3 cups chopped white onion</li><li>1/2 teaspoon dried red pepper flakes</li><li>1 tablespoon garlic powder</li><li>1/4 cup chili powder</li><li>2 (28 ounce) cans diced tomatoes</li><li>1 (16 ounce) can tomato sauce</li><li>1/2 cup gold tequila</li><li>1/2 cup orange juice</li><li>2 (15 ounce) cans chili beans in sauce</li></ul>	Heat the oil in a large pot over medium-high heat. Add the ground venison and cook, stirring to crumble, until no longer pink. Mix in the celery and onion; cook and stir until tender. Season with red pepper flakes, garlic powder and chili powder. Cook and stir for a minute to intensify the flavors. Pour in the tomatoes, tomato sauce, tequila and orange juice; simmer over low heat, uncovered, for 2 hours. After 2 hours, mix the beans into the chili and simmer for another 30 minutes.

Buffalo Chicken Chili

Ingredients	Directions
❖ 1 tablespoon extra-virgin olive oil ❖ 2 tablespoons butter ❖ 2 pounds ground chicken breast ❖ 1 large carrot, peeled and finely chopped ❖ 1 large onion, chopped ❖ 3 stalks celery, finely chopped ❖ 5 cloves garlic, chopped ❖ 5 tablespoons chili powder ❖ 2 tablespoons ground cumin ❖ 1 tablespoon ground paprika salt and pepper to taste ❖ 1/2 cup hot buffalo wing sauce (such as Frank'sB® REDHOT Buffalo Wing Sauce), or to taste ❖ 2 (15 ounce) cans tomato sauce ❖ 1 (15 ounce) can crushed tomatoes ❖ 1 (15 ounce) can white kidney or cannellini beans, drained ❖ 1 (19 ounce) can red kidney beans, drained	Heat olive oil and butter in a large pot over medium-high heat. Place chicken in the pot. Cook and stir 7 to 10 minutes, until chicken is no longer pink. Stir in the carrot, onion, celery, garlic, chili powder, cumin, paprika, and salt and pepper, and cook and stir until the onion is translucent and the vegetables are beginning to soften, 3 to 4 more minutes. Stir in the hot sauce, tomato sauce, crushed tomatoes, and white and red kidney beans. Bring to a boil, and simmer over medium-low heat about 1 hour, until the vegetables are tender and the flavors have blended.

Belly Burner Chili

Ingredients	Directions
❖ 3 pounds ground spicy pork sausage ❖ 2 cups chopped onion ❖ 3 (15 ounce) cans tomato sauce ❖ 3/4 cup water ❖ 1/2 cup chopped black olives ❖ 1/2 cup chopped green olives ❖ 1/2 teaspoon ground black pepper ❖ 1 tablespoon soy sauce ❖ 2 teaspoons chili powder ❖ 1 (15 ounce) can kidney beans	In a large skillet over medium-high heat, cook sausage until brown. Drain and crumble. In a slow cooker, combine sausage, onion, tomato sauce, water, black and green olives, pepper, soy sauce, chili powder and beans. Cover and cook on low 8 hours.

Dad's Chili

Ingredients	Directions
❖ 2 1/2 pounds ground beef ❖ 1 pound ground pork ❖ 1/2 cup butter ❖ 2 cloves garlic, diced ❖ 1 pound green bell pepper, chopped ❖ 1 1/2 pounds onion, chopped ❖ 2 (15 ounce) cans pinto beans, rinsed and drained ❖ 5 cups canned diced tomatoes with their juice ❖ 1/2 cup chopped fresh parsley ❖ 2 tablespoons chili powder, or more to taste ❖ 1 1/2 teaspoons ground black pepper ❖ 1 1/2 teaspoons monosodium glutamate (such as Ac'cent®) ❖ 1 tablespoon salt ❖ 1 1/2 teaspoons ground cumin	Heat a large skillet over medium-high heat and stir in the ground beef and ground pork. Cook and stir until the meat is crumbly, evenly browned, and no longer pink. Drain and discard any excess grease. Set meat aside. Melt the butter in the pot over medium heat. Stir in the garlic, bell pepper, and onion; cook and stir until the onion has softened and turned translucent, about 5 minutes. Stir in the cooked meat, pinto beans, tomatoes, parsley, chili powder, pepper, monosodium glutamate, salt, and cumin. Cover and bring to a boil, then reduce heat, and simmer for 1 hour.

Chili Mac

Ingredients	Directions
❖ 1 pound ground beef or turkey ❖ 1 medium onion, chopped ❖ 1 green bell pepper, chopped ❖ 1 (14.5 ounce) can Mexican or chili-style stewed tomatoes, undrained ❖ 1/2 cup water ❖ 1 (1.25 ounce) package taco seasoning mix ❖ 2 cups elbow macaroni or small shells, cooked and drained ❖ 2 cups Sargento ® Shredded Reduced Fat 4 Cheese Mexican Cheese, divided	Cook ground beef, onion and green pepper in large skillet over medium heat 5 minutes or until beef is no longer pink; pour off drippings. Add tomatoes, water and taco seasoning; simmer 5 minutes, stirring occasionally. Toss pasta with meat mixture. Spoon 3 cups of mixture into an 11x7-inch baking dish. Sprinkle with 1 cup cheese; top with remaining meat mixture. Cover with foil; bake in preheated 375 degrees F oven 30 minutes. Uncover; sprinkle with remaining cheese. Return to oven 5 minutes or until cheese is melted.

Chili Jack Chicken

Ingredients	Directions
❖ 2 skinless, boneless chicken breast halves ❖ 1 tablespoon butter or margarine ❖ 1 tablespoon vegetable oil 1/2 cup chicken broth ❖ 1 (4 ounce) can chopped green chilies ❖ 1 teaspoon prepared mustard ❖ 1 garlic clove, minced ❖ salt to taste ❖ 1/2 cup whipping cream ❖ 1/2 cup shredded Monterey Jack cheese ❖ Hot cooked rice	In a large skillet, brown chicken in butter an oil for 10 minutes; drain. Add the broth, chilies, mustard, garlic and salt. Simmer, uncovered, for 10 minutes or until chicken juices run clear. Stir in the cream; simmer until thickened. Sprinkle with cheese. Cover and cook until the cheese is melted. Serve over rice.

Cheesy Green Chili Rice

Ingredients	Directions
❖ 1 large onion, chopped ❖ 2 tablespoons butter or margarine ❖ 4 cups hot cooked long-grain rice ❖ 2 cups sour cream ❖ 1 cup small curd cottage cheese ❖ 1/2 teaspoon salt ❖ 1/8 teaspoon pepper ❖ 2 (4 ounce) cans chopped green chilies, drained ❖ 2 cups shredded Cheddar cheese	In a large skillet, cook onion in butter until tender. Remove from the heat. Stir in the rice, sour cream, cottage cheese, salt and pepper. Spoon half of the mixture into a greased 11-in. x 7-in. x 2-in. baking dish. Top with half of the chilies and cheese. Repeat layers. Bake, uncovered, at 375 degrees F for 20-25 minutes or until heated through and bubbly.

Mexican Chocolate Chili

Ingredients	Directions
❖ 1 pound ground round ❖ 1 cup chopped onion ❖ 1 cup hot water ❖ 2 (14.5 ounce) cans diced tomatoes with garlic, undrained ❖ 1 (15 ounce) can kidney beans, rinsed and drained ❖ 1 (15 ounce) can black beans, rinsed and drained ❖ 1 (14.5 ounce) can whole kernel corn, drained ❖ 1/3 cup semisweet chocolate chips ❖ 2 teaspoons chili powder ❖ 1 tablespoon ground cumin ❖ 1/2 teaspoon dried oregano ❖ 1 teaspoon salt	Combine ground round and onion in a large saucepan over medium-high heat. Cook, stirring, until beef is browned, about 5 minutes. Transfer cooked beef and onions to slow cooker. Stir in water, tomatoes, kidney beans, black beans, corn, chocolate chips, chili powder, cumin, oregano, and salt. Cook on High until chili begins to bubble, about 20 minutes. Reduce heat to Low, and cook until thick, about 2 hours

Spicy Chili Seasoning Mix

Ingredients	Directions
❖ 4 tablespoons chili powder ❖ 2 1/2 teaspoons ground coriander ❖ 2 1/2 teaspoons ground cumin ❖ 1 1/2 teaspoons garlic powder ❖ 1 teaspoon dried oregano ❖ 1/2 teaspoon cayenne pepper ADDITIONAL INGREDIENTS: ❖ 1 pound boneless round steak, cut into 1-inch cubes ❖ 2 teaspoons vegetable oil ❖ 1 pound lean ground beef ❖ 1 medium onion, chopped ❖ 1 (28 ounce) can diced tomatoes, undrained ❖ 2 (15 ounce) cans chili beans, divided	Combine the first six ingredients. Store in an airtight container in a cool dry place.

Easy Texas Chili

Ingredients	Directions
❖ 2 pounds lean ground beef ❖ 1 large onion, diced ❖ 1 large bell pepper, minced ❖ 3 (15 ounce) cans pinto beans ❖ 2 (28 ounce) cans diced tomatoes ❖ 4 (8 ounce) cans tomato sauce ❖ 3 jalapeno peppers, minced (optional) ❖ 1/2 cup chili powder ❖ 1 teaspoon crushed red pepper flakes ❖ 1 teaspoon ground black pepper 1/2 teaspoon salt ❖ 1/4 teaspoon garlic powder	Cook and stir the beef, onion, and bell pepper in a large pot over medium heat until the beef is brown and onion and pepper are tender, about 10 minutes. Drain grease from beef. Stir in beans, tomatoes, tomato sauce, jalapenos (if using), chili powder, red pepper flakes, black pepper, salt, and garlic powder. Bring mixture to a slow boil; cover and reduce heat. Simmer chili at least 30 minutes, stirring occasionally so that it does not stick. This chili can be simmered for several hours; the longer you simmer, the more flavor you will get.

Authentic Cincinnati Chili

Ingredients	Directions
❖ 2 pounds lean ground beef ❖ 1 quart water, or amount to cover ❖ 2 onions, finely chopped ❖ 1 (15 ounce) can tomato sauce ❖ 2 tablespoons vinegar ❖ 2 teaspoons Worcestershire sauce ❖ 4 cloves garlic, minced ❖ 1/2 (1 ounce) square unsweetened chocolate ❖ 1/4 cup chili powder ❖ 1 1/2 teaspoons salt ❖ 1 teaspoon ground cumin ❖ 1 teaspoon ground cinnamon ❖ 1/2 teaspoon ground cayenne pepper ❖ 5 whole cloves ❖ 5 whole allspice berries ❖ 1 bay leaf	Place the ground beef in a large pan, cover with about 1 quart of cold water, and bring to a boil, stirring and breaking up the beef with a fork to a fine texture. Slowly boil until the meat is thoroughly cooked, about 30 minutes, then remove from heat and refrigerate in the pan overnight. The next day, skim the solid fat from the top of the pan, and discard the fat. Place the beef mixture over medium heat, and stir in the onions, tomato sauce, vinegar, Worcestershire sauce, garlic, chocolate, chili powder, salt, cumin, cinnamon, cayenne pepper, cloves, allspice berries, and bay leaf. Bring to a boil, reduce heat to a simmer, and cook, stirring occasionally, for 3 hours. Add water if necessary to prevent the chili from burning.

Paprika Chili Steak

Ingredients	Directions
❖ 1 medium onion, chopped ❖ 1/2 cup ketchup ❖ 1/4 cup cider vinegar ❖ 1 tablespoon paprika ❖ 1 tablespoon canola oil ❖ 2 teaspoons chili powder ❖ 1 teaspoon salt ❖ 1/8 teaspoon pepper ❖ 1 1/2 pounds beef flank steak	In a large resealable plastic bag, combine the first eight ingredients; add steak. Seal bag and turn to coat; refrigerate for 3 hours or overnight, turning occasionally. Coat grill rack with nonstick cooking spray before starting the grill. Drain and discard marinade. Grill steak, covered, over medium-hot heat for 6-8 minutes on each side or until meat reaches desired doneness (for medium-rare, a meat thermometer should read 145 degrees F; medium, 160 degrees F, well-done, 170

	degrees F.

Shrimp Lollipops with Pineapple Chili Dipping

Ingredients	Directions
❖ For the Lollipops ❖ 8 Callisons Ginger Mango Seasoned Skewers (appetizer size) ❖ 8 ounces raw shrimp meat ❖ 1 tablespoon minced fresh ginger root ❖ 1 teaspoon minced garlic ❖ 1 tablespoon chopped fresh cilantro ❖ 2 teaspoons soy sauce ❖ 1 egg white ❖ 1 1/2 teaspoons cornstarch ❖ Pineapple Chili Dipping Sauce ❖ 1/3 cup finely chopped fresh pineapple ❖ 1/3 cup Asian sweet chili sauce Chopped fresh cilantro, for ❖ garnish	In a food processor fitted with a steel blade, add the shrimp meat, ginger, garlic, cilantro and soy sauce. In a small bowl, combine egg white and corn starch and whisk until frothy then add to the shrimp mixture. Pulse until chopped well. Cover and refrigerate mixture for 30 minutes. Meanwhile, make the Pineapple Chili Dipping Sauce; in a small bowl, combine chopped pineapple and chili sauce. Set aside. Preheat oven to 375 degrees F. To form and serve lollipops: for each skewer, form about 1 1/2 tablespoons of chilled shrimp mixture around the tip of each skewer forming a slightly oval shape. Place onto a lightly oiled baking sheet with sides not touching. Bake in preheated oven for about 10 to 12 minutes or until cooked through. Serve lollipops with the dipping sauce and garnish with chopped cilantro.

Chili Cheese Snacks

Ingredients	Directions
❖ 2 (3 ounce) packages cream cheese, softened ❖ 1 cup shredded Cheddar cheese ❖ 1/4 cup chopped green chiles ❖ 1/4 cup chopped ripe olives, drained ❖ 2 teaspoons dried minced onion ❖ 1/4 teaspoon hot pepper sauce ❖ 2 (8 ounce) cans refrigerated crescent rolls	In a small mixing bowl, beat cream cheese. Add the cheddar cheese, chilies, olives, onion and hot pepper sauce. Separate each tube of crescent dough into four rectangles; press perforations to seal. Spread cheese mixture over dough. Roll up jelly-roll style, starting with a long side. Cut each roll into 10 slices; place on greased baking sheets. Bake at 400 degrees F for 8-10 minutes or until golden brown.

Potatoes with Fresh Ginger and Chilies

Ingredients	Directions
❖ 4 large potatoes, peeled and diced ❖ 1/4 cup canola oil ❖ 2 teaspoons minced fresh ginger ❖ 1 green chile pepper, seeded and diced ❖ 1/2 teaspoon ground turmeric salt to taste ❖ 2 ripe tomatoes, peeled and chopped ❖ 1 tablespoon chopped fresh curry leaves	Place the potatoes in a large pot of salted water, and bring to a boil. Cook until tender but still firm, about 15 minutes. Drain, and cool.Heat the oil in a skillet over medium heat. Stir in the ginger and chile pepper; cook 2 minutes. Stir in the turmeric; cook 30 seconds. Combine the potatoes with the chile pepper mixture. Add salt as desired. Stir and cook 5 to 10 minutes more. Stir in the tomatoes and curry leaves; cook another 2 to 3 minutes. Serve immediately.

Golden Chili Chicken

Ingredients	Directions

Ingredients	Directions
❖ 2 tablespoons vegetable oil ❖ 1 (2 to 3 pound) whole chicken, cut into pieces ❖ 1 large onion, cut into 1/2-inch wide slices ❖ 3/4 cup orange juice ❖ 1 tablespoon dried parsley ❖ 1 teaspoon salt ❖ 1 tablespoon chili powder	In a small bowl, mix together orange juice, parsley, salt, and chili powder. Heat oil until hot in a 12-inch skillet over medium-high heat. Cook chicken pieces until browned on all sides. Remove excess fat from skillet. Add sliced onions and orange juice mixture to chicken in skillet. Heat to boiling, and then reduce heat to low. Cover. Simmer for 30 minutes, or until chicken is tender. Stir occasionally.

Chili For Two

Ingredients	Directions
❖ 1/4 pound ground beef ❖ 1/4 cup chopped onion ❖ 1 garlic clove, minced ❖ 1 (15.5 ounce) can chili beans, undrained ❖ 1 (14.5 ounce) can diced tomatoes, undrained ❖ 1 1/2 teaspoons chili powder 1/2 teaspoon ground cumin	In a saucepan, cook beef, onion and garlic over medium heat until meat is no longer pink; drain. Stir in the remaining ingredients; bring to a boil. Reduce heat; cover and simmer for 10-15 minutes or until heated through.

Nacho Chili

Ingredients	Directions
❖ 2 pounds lean ground beef ❖ 2 (14.5 ounce) cans stewed tomatoes ❖ 2 cups chopped celery ❖ 1 (16 ounce) jar salsa ❖ 1 (16 ounce) can kidney beans, rinsed and drained ❖ 1 (16 ounce) can refried beans ❖ 1 medium onion, chopped ❖ 1 cup water ❖ 1 (1.25 ounce) package taco seasoning ❖ 1/2 teaspoon pepper ❖ 1 (11 ounce) can condensed nacho cheese soup, undiluted	Crumble beef into a large bowl. Add the next nine ingredients and mix well. Transfer to a greased ovenproof Dutch oven or roasting pan. Cover and bake at 350 degrees F for 1 hour or until the meat is no longer pink, stirring once. Let stand for 5 minutes. Garnish individual servings with a dollop of cheese soup.

Vegetarian Black Bean Chili

Ingredients	Directions
❖ 1/2 cup applesauce ❖ 1 tablespoon brown sugar ❖ 1 tablespoon ground coriander ❖ 1 teaspoon ground cayenne pepper ❖ 1 teaspoon ground cumin ❖ 1 teaspoon dried oregano ❖ 1/2 teaspoon ground cloves ❖ 1/2 teaspoon dried rosemary ❖ 1/2 teaspoon dried sage ❖ 1/4 teaspoon dried thyme ❖ 1 pinch asafoetida powder (optional) ❖ 1 (15 ounce) can black beans ❖ 1 (6 ounce) can tomato paste ❖ 2 cloves garlic, minced ❖ 1 onion, chopped ❖ 1 yellow squash, chopped	In a large pot over medium-low heat, mix the applesauce, brown sugar, coriander, cayenne pepper, cumin, oregano, cloves, rosemary, sage, thyme and asafoetida powder. Cook just until heated through. Stir in black beans and tomato paste. Mix in garlic, onion, squash, carrots, sweet potato and mushrooms. Pour in enough water to cover. Bring to a boil, reduce heat to low and simmer 45 minutes, stirring occasionally.

❖ 2 carrots, chopped	
❖ 1 sweet potato, peeled and diced	
❖ 1 cup chopped fresh mushrooms	
❖ 1 quart water, or as needed	

Beef, Green Chili and Tomato Stew

Ingredients	Directions
❖ 1/4 cup vegetable oil ❖ 3 pounds beef chuck roast, cut into 3/4 inch cubes ❖ 2 onions, chopped ❖ 2 cloves garlic, minced ❖ 1 (28 ounce) can roma tomatoes, with juice ❖ 2 (4 ounce) cans chopped green chile peppers, drained ❖ 1 (12 fluid ounce) can or bottle beer ❖ 1 cup beef broth ❖ 2 teaspoons dried oregano, crushed ❖ 1 1/2 teaspoons ground cumin ❖ 2 tablespoons Worcestershire sauce ❖ salt to taste ground black pepper to taste	In a Dutch oven, heat oil over medium heat until hot, but not smoking. Pat the meat dry with paper towels and brown in batches, transferring the meat with a slotted spoon to a bowl as they are done. In the fat remaining in the pot, cook the onions until softened, about 5 minutes. Stir in the garlic and cook for 1 more minute. Return meat to the pot with any juices in the bowl and add the tomatoes with juice, chiles, beer, beef broth, oregano, cumin, and Worcestershire sauce. Season with salt and pepper to taste. Bring to a boil and reduce heat. Simmer, partially covered, for 2 1/2 hours or until meat is tender.

Colorado Green Chili (Chile Verde)

Ingredients	Directions
❖ 1 tablespoon olive oil ❖ 1 1/2 pounds cubed pork stew meat ❖ salt and pepper to taste ❖ 1 large yellow onion, diced ❖ 4 cloves garlic, minced ❖ 2 cups chopped, roasted green chiles ❖ 1 (14.5 ounce) can diced tomatoes with juice ❖ 1 1/2 cups tomatillo salsa ❖ 5 cups chicken broth ❖ 1/2 teaspoon dried oregano ❖ 1 pinch ground cloves	Heat the olive oil in a Dutch oven or large pot over medium-high heat. Season the pork with salt and pepper to taste, then place into the hot oil. Cook until golden brown on all sides, about 7 minutes. Once browned, remove the pork and set aside. Reduce heat to medium, and stir in the onion and garlic. Cook and stir until the onion has softened and turned translucent, about 5 minutes. Return the pork to the pot, and stir in the green chiles, diced tomatoes with juice, tomatillo salsa, and chicken broth. Season with oregano and clove. Bring to a simmer over medium-high heat, then reduce heat to medium-low, cover, and simmer 20 minutes. After 20 minutes, remove 2 cups of the soup (ensure there are no pork cubes in it), and pour into a blender. Hold down the lid of the blender with a folded kitchen towel, and carefully start the blender, using a few quick pulses to get the soup moving before leaving it on to puree. Puree until smooth, and then pour back into the cooking pot. This will create a thicker texture for your chili and will eliminate some of the chunky bits of chiles. Continue to simmer, stirring occasionally until the pork is very tender, at least 35 minutes more.

Chili II

Ingredients	Directions
❖ 2 pounds ground beef ❖ 1 onion, chopped ❖ 2 (16 ounce) cans chili beans ❖ 1 (15 ounce) can tomato sauce ❖ 1 (10 ounce) can diced tomatoes with green chile peppers ❖ 1 (14.5 ounce) can peeled and diced tomatoes ❖ 11 1/2 fluid ounces tomato juice ❖ 1 (4 ounce) can diced green chiles ❖ 1 (1.25 ounce) package chili seasoning mix	Cook ground beef and onion until done. In slow cooker or Dutch oven add all ingredients together. Simmer several hours.

Corn with Bacon and Chili Powder

Ingredients	Directions
❖ 4 ears corn, husked and cleaned ❖ 4 slices bacon ❖ 4 dashes chili powder	Wash the husked corn. Wrap one slice of bacon around each ear. It probably won't cover the entire ear, but be sure it goes from one end to the other. Sprinkle with chili powder to taste. Wrap the corn and bacon and chili powder in heavy aluminum foil and place over medium coals, or medium flame on gas grill. Cook approximately 20-25 minutes. Time will depend on the size of the ears of corn, and how fresh they are.

The Best Vegetarian Chili in the World

Ingredients	Directions
❖ 1 tablespoon olive oil ❖ 1/2 medium onion, chopped ❖ 2 bay leaves ❖ 1 teaspoon ground cumin ❖ 2 tablespoons dried oregano ❖ 1 tablespoon salt ❖ 2 stalks celery, chopped ❖ 2 green bell peppers, chopped ❖ 2 jalapeno peppers, chopped ❖ 3 cloves garlic, chopped ❖ 2 (4 ounce) cans chopped green chile peppers, drained ❖ 2 (12 ounce) packages vegetarian burger crumbles ❖ 3 (28 ounce) cans whole peeled tomatoes, crushed ❖ 1/4 cup chili powder ❖ 1 tablespoon ground black pepper ❖ 1 (15 ounce) can kidney beans, drained ❖ 1 (15 ounce) can garbanzo beans, drained ❖ 1 (15 ounce) can black beans ❖ 1 (15 ounce) can whole kernel corn	Heat the olive oil in a large pot over medium heat. Stir in the onion, and season with bay leaves, cumin, oregano, and salt. Cook and stir until onion is tender, then mix in the celery, green bell peppers, jalapeno peppers, garlic, and green chile peppers. When vegetables are heated through, mix in the vegetarian burger crumbles. Reduce heat to low, cover pot, and simmer 5 minutes. Mix the tomatoes into the pot. Season chili with chili powder and pepper. Stir in the kidney beans, garbanzo beans, and black beans. Bring to a boil, reduce heat to low, and simmer 45 minutes. Stir in the corn, and continue cooking 5 minutes before serving.

Pinto Bean Chili

Ingredients	Directions
❖ 1 pound dried pinto beans ❖ 2 pounds ground beef ❖ 1 medium onion, chopped ❖ 3 celery ribs, chopped ❖ 3 tablespoons all-purpose flour ❖ 4 cups water ❖ 2 tablespoons chili powder ❖ 2 tablespoons ground cumin ❖ 1/2 teaspoon sugar ❖ 1 (28 ounce) can crushed tomatoes ❖ 2 teaspoons cider vinegar ❖ 1 1/2 teaspoons salt ❖ CHILI CHEESE QUESADILLAS: ❖ 2 (4 ounce) cans chopped green chilies ❖ 12 (6 inch) flour tortillas ❖ 3 cups shredded Cheddar cheese ❖ 3 teaspoons vegetable oil	Place beans in a Dutch oven or soup kettle; add water to cover by 2 in. Bring to a boil; boil for 2 minutes. Remove from the heat; cover and let stand for 1 hour. Drain and rinse beans, discarding liquid. In a Dutch oven, cook the beef, onion and celery over medium heat until meat is no longer pink; drain. Stir in flour until blended.Gradually stir in water. Add the beans, chili powder, cumin and sugar. Bring to a boil. Reduce heat; cover and simmer for 1-1/2 hours or until beans are tender. Stir in the tomatoes, vinegar and salt; heat through, stirring occasionally. Meanwhile, for quesadillas, spread about 1 tablespoon of chilies on half of each tortilla. Sprinkle with 1/4 cup of cheese; fold in half. In a large skillet, cook tortillas in 1 teaspoon of oil over medium heat until lightly browned on each side, adding more oil as needed. Cut each in half. Serve with chili.

Boilermaker Tailgate Chili

Ingredients	Directions
❖ 2 pounds ground beef chuck ❖ 1 pound bulk Italian sausage ❖ 3 (15 ounce) cans chili beans, drained ❖ 1 (15 ounce) can chili beans in spicy sauce ❖ 2 (28 ounce) cans diced tomatoes with juice ❖ 1 (6 ounce) can tomato paste ❖ 1 large yellow onion, chopped	Heat a large stock pot over medium-high heat. Crumble the ground chuck and sausage into the hot pan, and cook until evenly browned. Drain off excess grease. Pour in the chili beans, spicy chili beans, diced tomatoes and tomato paste. Add the onion, celery, green and red bell peppers, chile peppers, bacon bits, bouillon, and beer. Season with chili

- ❖ 3 stalks celery, chopped
- ❖ 1 green bell pepper, seeded and chopped
- ❖ 1 red bell pepper, seeded and chopped
- ❖ 2 green chile peppers, seeded and chopped
- ❖ 1 tablespoon bacon bits
- ❖ 4 cubes beef bouillon
- ❖ 1/2 cup beer
- ❖ 1/4 cup chili powder
- ❖ 1 tablespoon Worcestershire sauce
- ❖ 1 tablespoon minced garlic
- ❖ 1 tablespoon dried oregano
- ❖ 2 teaspoons ground cumin
- ❖ 2 teaspoons hot pepper sauce (e.
- ❖ g. Tabasco®„ў)
- ❖ 1 teaspoon dried basil
- ❖ 1 teaspoon salt
- ❖ 1 teaspoon ground black pepper
- ❖ 1 teaspoon cayenne pepper
- ❖ 1 teaspoon paprika
- ❖ 1 teaspoon white sugar
- ❖ 1 (10.5 ounce) bag corn chips such as FritosB®
- ❖ 1 (8 ounce) package shredded Cheddar cheese

powder, Worcestershire sauce, garlic, oregano, cumin, hot pepper sauce, basil, salt, pepper, cayenne, paprika, and sugar. Stir to blend, then cover and simmer over low heat for at least 2 hours, stirring occasionally.

After 2 hours, taste, and adjust salt, pepper, and chili powder if necessary. The longer the chili simmers, the better it will taste. Remove from heat and serve, or refrigerate, and serve the next day. To serve, ladle into bowls, and top with corn chips and shredded Cheddar cheese.

Bold Vegan Chili

Ingredients	Directions
❖ 1 (12 ounce) package vegetarian burger crumbles ❖ 3 (15.25 ounce) cans kidney beans ❖ 1 large red onion, chopped ❖ 4 stalks celery, diced ❖ 2 red bell peppers, chopped ❖ 4 bay leaves ❖ 2 tablespoons hot chili powder ❖ 3 tablespoons molasses ❖ 1 cube vegetable bouillon ❖ 1 tablespoon chopped fresh cilantro ❖ 1 teaspoon hot pepper sauce salt and pepper to taste ❖ 1 cup water ❖ 3 tablespoons all-purpose flour ❖ 1 cup hot water	In a slow cooker combine vegetarian crumbles, kidney beans, onion, celery, bell pepper, bay leaves, chili powder, molasses, bouillon, cilantro, hot sauce, salt, pepper and 1 cup water. Cook on high for 3 hours. Dissolve flour in 1 cup hot water. Pour into chili and cook 1 more an hour.

DB's Seven Pepper Chili

Ingredients	Directions
❖ 2 pounds beef tip ❖ 1 (18 ounce) bottle barbeque sauce ❖ 1 large onion, chopped ❖ 1 large green bell pepper, diced ❖ 2 tablespoons diced habanero pepper ❖ 2 pepperoncini, diced ❖ 1 tablespoon diced serrano pepper ❖ 1 tablespoon diced fresh cayenne pepper ❖ 1 tablespoon diced pequin chile pepper ❖ 2 tablespoons diced jalapeno	Preheat an outdoor grill for high heat and lightly oil grate. Brush beef tip with barbeque sauce and grill 5 to 8 minutes on a side, or to desired doneness, brushing frequently with sauce. Set aside. In a large pot over medium heat, cook onion and bell, habanero, pepperoncini, serrano, cayenne, pequin and jalapeno peppers until onion is translucent. Stir in cumin, paprika, oregano and chili powder and cook until fragrant. Stir in ground beef and cook until brown. Drain. Stir in tomato sauce, any remaining barbeque sauce and beans. Cut grilled

Ingredients	Directions
chile pepper ❖ 1 teaspoon crushed red pepper flakes ❖ 1 teaspoon ground cumin ❖ 1 teaspoon paprika ❖ 1 teaspoon dried oregano ❖ 3 tablespoons chili powder ❖ 2 pounds ground beef ❖ 1 (14.5 ounce) can crushed tomatoes ❖ 1 (15 ounce) can pinto beans, drained	tip steak into bite sized pieces and stir into chili as well. Continue to cook until thickened and flavors have blended and mixture is thoroughly heated. Thin with water if desired.

Chili Chicken I

Ingredients	Directions
❖ 4 (4 ounce) skinless, boneless chicken breast halves ❖ 1/4 pound butter ❖ 2 cloves garlic, chopped ❖ 1 teaspoon ground black pepper ❖ 3 teaspoons chili powder ❖ 1/2 cup lemon juice ❖ 1/4 teaspoon lemon zest ❖ 3 teaspoons Worcestershire sauce ❖ 1 (29 ounce) can peach halves, drained	Preheat oven to 350 degrees F (175 degrees C). Melt butter or margarine in a large saucepan. Add garlic, pepper, chili powder, lemon juice, lemon rind and Worcestershire sauce. Mix well. Place chicken in a lightly greased 9x13 inch baking dish. Pour butter/margarine mixture over chicken, cover dish and bake in the preheated oven for 45 minutes or until thick parts of chicken are tender and juices run clear. Arrange peach halves around chicken and spoon a little sauce over the peaches. Broil for 5 minutes and serve.

Chili IV

Ingredients	Directions
❖ 1 1/2 pounds ground beef ❖ 1 tablespoon vegetable oil ❖ 1/2 teaspoon salt ❖ 1 (10.5 ounce) can condensed French onion soup ❖ 1 tablespoon chili powder ❖ 2 teaspoons ground cumin ❖ 1/2 teaspoon ground black pepper ❖ 1 (6 ounce) can tomato paste ❖ 1 (8 ounce) can tomato sauce ❖ 2 (15 ounce) cans kidney beans ❖ 2 teaspoons unsweetened cocoa ❖ 1 cup cola-flavored carbonated beverage	In a deep skillet or large saucepan, cook beef with oil and salt over medium heat until brown. Meanwhile, puree French onion soup in a blender until smooth. Drain meat. Stir pureed soup into meat, reduce heat and simmer 5 minutes. Stir in chili powder, cumin, pepper, tomato paste, tomato sauce, and beans until well combined. Stir in cocoa and cola. Heat through and serve.

West Texas-Style Buffalo Chili

Ingredients	Directions
❖ 1 (8 ounce) package dry black beans ❖ 1 (8 ounce) package dry kidney beans ❖ 1 tablespoon chili powder ❖ 1/2 teaspoon crushed red pepper flakes ❖ salt and pepper to taste ❖ 1 jalapeno pepper, seeded and minced ❖ 2 tablespoons vegetable oil ❖ 1 large sweet onion, chopped ❖ 2 green bell peppers, chopped ❖ 2 zucchini, diced ❖ 3 (10 ounce) cans diced tomatoes with green chile peppers ❖ 1 (10 ounce) can tomato sauce ❖ 1/2 (16 ounce) jar hot chunky	Soak beans in water overnight. Drain and rinse. In a large pot, combine beans with water to cover. Bring to a boil, reduce heat, and simmer 1 to 2 hours, until tender. Once the beans have absorbed most of the water, and are starting to soften, season with chile powder, red pepper flakes, jalapeno, salt and pepper. Reserve the seeds. Heat oil in a large heavy skillet over medium low heat. Saute the onion and bell peppers for 3 minutes. Stir in diced zucchini, diced tomatoes, tomato sauce and salsa. Season with jalapeno seeds and chili sauce, stir well, and leave on medium-low heat. Place ground buffalo meat in a large,

	salsa ❖ 2 tablespoons chili sauce ❖ 2 pounds ground buffalo	deep skillet. Cook over medium high heat until evenly brown. Drain excess fat. Stir buffalo and vegetable mixture into beans. Continue to simmer for 1 hour.

Unbelievably Easy and Delicious Vegetarian Chili

Ingredients	Directions
❖ 1 (28 ounce) can diced tomatoes with juice ❖ 1 small onion, diced ❖ 1 (15 ounce) can white beans, drained ❖ 1 (15 ounce) can chili beans, with liquid ❖ 1 (1.25 ounce) package reduced sodium taco seasoning mix ❖ 1 (1 ounce) package ranch dressing mix ❖ 1 (12 ounce) package vegetarian burger crumbles ❖ 1 (8 ounce) package shredded Cheddar cheese (optional)	Mix the tomatoes, onion, white beans, chili beans, taco seasoning mix, and ranch dressing mix in a large pot over medium heat. Bring to a boil. Reduce heat to low, mix in the burger crumbles, and continue cooking until heated through. Top with cheese to serve.

Slow Cooker Sweet Chicken Chili

Ingredients	Directions
❖ 6 skinless, boneless chicken breast halves ❖ 1 (15 ounce) can dark red kidney beans, undrained ❖ 1 (15 ounce) can pinto beans, undrained ❖ 1 (15 ounce) can black beans, undrained ❖ 2 onions, cut into chunks ❖ 1 green bell pepper, coarsely chopped ❖ 1 (6 ounce) can tomato paste	Place the chicken breasts into a slow cooker, and pour in the kidney beans, pinto beans, black beans, onions, green bell pepper, tomato paste, brown sugar, rice vinegar, chili black bean sauce, and sea salt. Stir to combine all ingredients, and set the cooker to High. Cook for 1 hour; stir again, and set the cooker to Low. Cook for 4 more hours. Remove the chicken breasts, shred with 2 forks, and stir the shredded chicken back into the chili. Sprinkle the top of the chili with Cheddar cheese, and serve.

- ❖ 1/3 cup brown sugar
- ❖ 2 tablespoons seasoned rice vinegar
- ❖ 1 tablespoon Asian chili black bean sauce
- ❖ 1/2 teaspoon sea salt
- ❖ 1/2 cup shredded Cheddar cheese

Carne Con Chilies

Ingredients	Directions
❖ 4 large boneless pork chops, fat trimmed and reserved ❖ 1/4 teaspoon ground black pepper, or to taste ❖ 1/2 teaspoon garlic powder, or to taste ❖ 1/2 teaspoon seasoning salt, or to taste ❖ 1 lime, cut into 4 wedges ❖ 10 tomatillos, husked and cut in half ❖ 1 tomato, quartered ❖ 2 jalapeno peppers, seeded and halved ❖ 3 dried red chile peppers, chopped ❖ 1 clove garlic ❖ 1/2 teaspoon salt, or to taste	Slice pork chops into strips, and season with pepper, garlic powder and seasoning salt. Squeeze lime juice over pieces. Heat a skillet over medium heat. Add fat, and cook, stirring until pan is coated. Remove fat, and put the seasoned meat in the pan. Fry until browned, about 5 minutes. At the same time, make the green sauce. Combine the tomatillos, tomato, jalapenos, and dried chilies in a saucepan. Bring to a boil, and cook until soft. Drain excess liquid, and transfer to a blender or food processor along with the garlic and salt. Blend until smooth. Pour sauce over the meat in the pan, and simmer for 15 minutes to blend all of the flavors. Taste, and adjust salt and pepper if necessary.

Chili Stew

Ingredients	Directions
❖ 1 pound ground beef ❖ 1 medium onion, chopped ❖ 1 small green pepper, chopped ❖ 2 (15 ounce) cans spicy chili beans ❖ 1 (16 ounce) can kidney beans, rinsed and drained ❖ 1 (15.25 ounce) can whole kernel corn, drained ❖ 1 (14.5 ounce) can diced tomatoes with garlic and onion ❖ 1 (8 ounce) can tomato sauce ❖ 1 (4 ounce) can chopped green chilies ❖ 2 tablespoons chili powder ❖ 1/2 teaspoon salt	In a Dutch oven or large saucepan, cook the beef, onion and green pepper over medium heat until meat is no longer pink; drain. Stir in remaining ingredients. Bring to a boil. Reduce heat; simmer, uncovered, for 15 minutes, stirring occasionally.

Chili Casserole

Ingredients	Directions
❖ 1/2 pound macaroni, cooked ❖ 1 (15 ounce) can chili with beans ❖ 1 (15 ounce) can sweet corn, drained ❖ 1/2 pound ground beef, browned and drained ❖ 2 tablespoons hot sauce ❖ 1/2 cup chopped onion ❖ 1 tablespoon chili seasoning mix ❖ 1/2 cup shredded mozzarella cheese	Preheat oven to 300 degrees F (150 degrees C). In a large bowl, combine the macaroni, chili, corn, beef, hot sauce, onion, seasoning mix and cheese. Mix well and spread mixture into a 9x13 inch baking dish. Bake in the preheated oven for 20 minutes, or until heated through.

Sharon's Awesome Chicago Chili

Ingredients	Directions
❖ 2 pounds ground beef ❖ 4 (14.5 ounce) cans kidney beans ❖ 4 (15 ounce) cans diced tomatoes ❖ 1 (12 fluid ounce) bottle beer ❖ 1 (12 ounce) bottle tomato-based chili sauce ❖ 1 large white onion, chopped ❖ 6 cloves garlic, minced ❖ 2 tablespoons chili seasoning ❖ 1 teaspoon black pepper ❖ 1/2 teaspoon garlic powder ❖ 1/2 teaspoon onion powder ❖ 1/2 teaspoon cayenne pepper ❖ 1/2 teaspoon oregano ❖ 1/4 cup sugar ❖ 1 teaspoon hot sauce ❖ 1 teaspoon Worcestershire sauce	Place the ground beef in a large pot and cook over medium heat until evenly brown. Drain off the excess fat. Mix in the kidney beans, diced tomatoes, beer, chili sauce, onion, garlic, chili seasoning, black pepper, garlic powder, onion, cayenne pepper, oregano, sugar, hot sauce, and Worcestershire sauce. Bring to a boil. Reduce heat to low, and simmer for about 4 hours, stirring occasionally.

Green Enchilada Pork Chili

Ingredients	Directions
❖ 4 tablespoons olive oil, divided ❖ 1 pound ground pork ❖ 2 fresh jalapeno peppers, stems removed ❖ 1 tablespoon butter ❖ 1 medium white onion, diced ❖ 1 teaspoon kosher salt ❖ 1/2 teaspoon ground cumin ❖ 1/2 teaspoon sweet paprika ❖ 1/4 teaspoon ground cayenne pepper ❖ 1/4 teaspoon ground black pepper ❖ 3 cloves garlic, minced ❖ 1/2 cup all-purpose flour ❖ 1 (28 ounce) can green enchilada	In a 4 quart pot, heat 2 tablespoons olive oil over medium heat. Add the jalapenos and saute for 1 minute. Stir in the ground pork and cook until evenly brown. Remove the browned pork and jalapenos from the pot and set aside. In the same pot used to cook the meat, add the remaining 2 tablespoons olive oil, butter, and onion. Cook for 2 minutes or until the onion starts to soften. Stir in the salt, cumin, paprika, cayenne, and black pepper and cook until the onion is soft. Mix in the garlic and cook for 1 minute. Reduce the heat to low. Sprinkle the flour over the onion and garlic. Cook, stirring for

sauce
- 1 (7 ounce) can green salsa
- 1 quart water
- 1/2 bunch fresh cilantro, chopped
  1/2 lime, juiced

three minutes. Slowly pour the enchilada sauce into the onion mixture, whisking constantly to prevent lumps from forming. Mix in the green salsa and water.

Return the cooked pork and jalapenos to the pot. Increase the heat to medium and slowly bring the soup to a boil. When the soup boils, reduce the heat and simmer for 30 minutes. Before serving remove from heat and stir in chopped cilantro and lime juice

Cincinnati Chili I

Ingredients	Directions
<ul><li>1 tablespoon vegetable oil</li><li>1/2 cup chopped onion</li><li>2 pounds ground beef</li><li>1/4 cup chili powder</li><li>1 teaspoon ground cinnamon</li><li>1 teaspoon ground cumin</li><li>1/4 teaspoon ground allspice</li><li>1/4 teaspoon ground cloves</li><li>1 bay leaf</li><li>1/2 (1 ounce) square unsweetened chocolate</li><li>2 (10.5 ounce) cans beef broth</li><li>1 (15 ounce) can tomato sauce</li><li>2 tablespoons cider vinegar</li><li>1/4 teaspoon ground cayenne pepper</li><li>1/4 cup shredded Cheddar cheese</li></ul>	Heat oil in a large saucepan over medium heat. Add onion and cook, stirring frequently, until tender, about 6 minutes. Add beef, in batches if necessary, and cook, breaking up with a wooden spoon, until browned. Add chili powder, cinnamon, cumin, allspice, cloves, bay leaf, chocolate, beef broth, tomato sauce, cider vinegar, and red pepper. Stir to mix well. Bring to a boil. Reduce heat to low; cover and simmer 1 1/2 hours, stirring occasionally. It is the best if you now refrigerate overnight. Remove the bay leaf. Reheat gently over medium heat. Serve over hot, drained spaghetti. Top with shredded cheddar cheese.

Corn Chili

Ingredients	Directions
❖ 2 tablespoons vegetable oil ❖ 1 onion, diced ❖ 1 teaspoon ground cayenne pepper ❖ 2 teaspoons dried oregano ❖ 1 pound frozen corn kernels ❖ 2 (14.5 ounce) cans Mexican-style stewed tomatoes ❖ 1 (15 ounce) can pinto beans, drained ❖ 1 (15 ounce) can kidney beans, drained ❖ 2 teaspoons chicken bouillon granules ❖ 1 cup water ❖ 1/2 teaspoon salt ❖ 1/4 teaspoon ground black pepper ❖ 1 1/2 cups tomato sauce ❖ 2 tablespoons tomato paste	In a large pot, cook onion in oil over medium heat 1 minute. Stir in cayenne and oregano and cook 1 minute more. Stir in corn, tomatoes, pinto beans, kidney beans, chicken bouillon granules, water, salt, pepper, tomato sauce and tomato paste. Cook, uncovered, until heated through and slightly thickened, 10 to 15 minutes.

Best Yet Turkey Chili

Ingredients	Directions
❖ 1 1/2 pounds ground turkey ❖ 1 green bell pepper, chopped ❖ 1 (19 ounce) can black beans, with liquid ❖ 1 (28 ounce) can diced tomatoes, with liquid ❖ 1 (15.25 ounce) can whole kernel corn, with liquid ❖ 1 pinch ground cumin, or to taste ❖ 1 pinch chili powder, or to taste ❖ 1 pinch red pepper flakes, or to taste ❖ 1 pinch ground cinnamon, or to taste	Place turkey and bell pepper in a large saucepan over medium heat, and cook until turkey is evenly brown. Mix in beans, tomatoes, and corn. Season with cumin, chili powder, red pepper flakes, and cinnamon. Bring to a boil, reduce heat to low, and simmer 30 minutes. Add water if you want a more liquid chili.

Taste of Home's Double Chili Cheese Dip

Ingredients	Directions
❖ 1 (8 ounce) package light cream cheese, softened ❖ 1 (15 ounce) can turkey chili without beans ❖ 4 green onions, thinly sliced ❖ 3 tablespoons chopped green chilies ❖ 1/4 cup sliced ripe olives (optional) ❖ 1 cup shredded reduced-fat Cheddar cheese ❖ Baked tortilla chips	Spread cream cheese into a 9-in. pie plate or quiche dish that has been coated with nonstick cooking spray. Top with chili, onions, chilies and olives if desired. Sprinkle with cheese. Bake, uncovered, at 350 degrees for 15-20 minutes or until the cheese is melted. Serve with tortilla chips.

Green Chili Casserole

Ingredients	Directions
❖ 2 (7 ounce) cans whole green chile peppers, drained ❖ 1 1/2 cups shredded Cheddar cheese, divided ❖ 1/3 cup milk ❖ 4 eggs, lightly beaten salt and pepper to taste	Preheat oven to 350 degrees F (175 degrees C). Grease an 8x12 inch baking dish. Line the bottom of dish with green chiles. Sprinkle with 1/2 cup shredded cheese. Repeat layers twice more. In a medium bowl, whisk together milk and eggs. Season with salt and pepper. Pour egg mixture over chiles and cheese. Bake in preheated oven for 25 to 30 minutes, or until filling is set. Let stand 5 to 10 minutes before serving

Vegetarian Chili

Ingredients	Directions
❖ 2 (15 ounce) cans pinto beans, drained and rinsed ❖ 1 (28 ounce) can crushed tomatoes ❖ 1 (16 ounce) can kidney beans, rinsed and drained ❖ 1 (15 ounce) can yellow hominy, drained ❖ 1 (6 ounce) can tomato paste ❖ 1 (4 ounce) can chopped green chilies ❖ 2 small zucchini, halved and thinly sliced ❖ 1 medium onion, chopped ❖ 1 1/2 cups water ❖ 1 tablespoon chili powder ❖ 1 teaspoon ground cumin ❖ 1 teaspoon salt ❖ 1/2 teaspoon garlic powder ❖ 1/2 teaspoon sugar ❖ 1/2 cup shredded Monterey Jack	In a large kettle or Dutch oven, combine the first 15 ingredients; mix well. Bring to a boil. Reduce heat; cover and simmer for 30-35 minutes. Sprinkle with cheese.

cheese	

Chili Casserole

Ingredients	Directions
❖ 1 1/2 pounds ground beef ❖ 1/2 cup chopped onion ❖ 3 stalks celery, chopped ❖ 1 (15 ounce) can chili ❖ 1 (14.5 ounce) can peeled and diced tomatoes with juice ❖ 1/4 cup taco sauce ❖ 1 (15 ounce) can corn ❖ 1 (8 ounce) package egg noodles ❖ 1/4 cup shredded Cheddar ❖ cheese	Preheat oven to 350 degrees F (175 degrees C). In a large skillet over medium high heat, saute the beef and onion for 5 to 10 minutes, or until meat is browned and onion is tender; drain fat. Add the celery, chili, tomatoes, taco sauce and corn. Heat thoroughly, reduce heat to low and allow to simmer. Meanwhile, prepare the noodles according to package directions. When cooked, place them in a 9x13 inch baking dish. Pour the meat mixture over the noodles, stirring well. Top with the cheese. Bake at 350 degrees F (175 degrees C) for 20 minutes, or until cheese is completely melted and bubbly.

Chili Cheese Dip III

Ingredients	Directions
❖ 2 (8 ounce) packages cream cheese, softened ❖ 1 (15 ounce) can chili without beans ❖ 16 ounces shredded Cheddar cheese ❖ 1 (13.5 ounce) package nacho-flavor tortilla chips	Spread cream cheese on the bottom of a microwave-safe dish. Spread a layer of chili over the cream cheese. Finish with a layer of shredded cheddar cheese. Microwave for 5 minutes or until the cheese melts. Serve with spicy nacho tortilla chips.

Diann's Chili Vegetable Soup

Ingredients	Directions
❖ 2 pounds ground beef ❖ 6 stalks celery, chopped ❖ 2 onion, chopped ❖ 1 green bell pepper, chopped ❖ 1 small head cabbage, chopped ❖ 3 (15 ounce) cans kidney beans ❖ 46 ounces tomato-vegetable juice cocktail ❖ 1 (46 fluid ounce) can tomato juice ❖ 2 (15 ounce) cans whole kernel corn, drained ❖ 4 (14.5 ounce) cans diced tomatoes ❖ 3 tablespoons chili powder ❖ 1/4 tablespoon garlic powder salt and pepper to taste	In a large soup pot, saute ground beef until brown. Drain excess fat. Add celery, onions, green bell peppers, cabbage, kidney beans, vegetable juice, tomato juice, corn, diced tomatoes and chili powder. Bring to a boil, and then reduce heat to low. Cover pot and let simmer about one hour, or until celery is tender. Add garlic powder and salt and pepper to taste.

Amateur's Light Breeze Chicken Chili

Ingredients	Directions
❖ 2 (10 ounce) cans chunk chicken, undrained ❖ 2 (16 ounce) cans chili beans, drained ❖ 3 (14.5 ounce) cans Mexican-style stewed tomatoes ❖ 1 (12 ounce) jar sliced jalapeno peppers ❖ 1 large onion, chopped ❖ 2 large green bell peppers, seeded and chopped ❖ 1 1/2 tablespoons chili powder ❖ 2 tablespoons ground cumin ❖ 10 cups water, or as needed ❖ 1 (14.5 ounce) can chicken broth salt to taste	In a large stockpot, combine the chicken, chili beans, tomatoes, jalapenos, onion and green bell pepper. Season with chili powder and cumin. Pour in the chicken broth, and enough water to cover the ingredients. Stir well, and bring to a boil. Reduce heat tomedium, and let simmer for one hour. Season with salt to taste.

Quick Zesty Chili

Ingredients	Directions
❖ 1 pound ground beef ❖ 2 (15.5 ounce) cans kidney beans, rinsed and drained ❖ 1 (8 ounce) can tomato sauce ❖ 2 cups chopped fresh tomatoes ❖ 1 cup water ❖ 2 tablespoons chili powder ❖ 1 tablespoon dried minced onion ❖ 1 teaspoon hot pepper sauce ❖ 1 teaspoon ground cumin ❖ 1/4 teaspoon ground cinnamon	In a large saucepan, brown beef; drain. Add remaining ingredients. Bring to a boil; reduce heat and simmer for 15 minutes.

Lentil Chili

Ingredients	Directions
❖ 1 pound lean ground turkey ❖ 1 (49.5 fluid ounce) can reduced-sodium chicken broth ❖ 2 cups lentils, rinsed ❖ 1 (15 ounce) can tomato sauce ❖ 1 (14.5 ounce) can diced tomatoes, undrained ❖ 1 medium onion, chopped ❖ 1 tablespoon chili powder ❖ 1 teaspoon ground cumin ❖ 1/4 teaspoon pepper	In a Dutch oven, cook turkey over medium heat until no longer pink; drain. Add the remaining ingredients; bring to a boil. Reduce heat; cover and simmer for 25-30 minutes or until lentils are tender.

Portobello Mushroom Chili

Ingredients	Directions
❖ 2 tablespoons extra virgin olive oil ❖ 2 medium onions, diced ❖ 2 cloves garlic, chopped ❖ 1 tablespoon chili powder	Heat the oil in a large pot over medium heat, and cook the onions until tender. Stir in the garlic, chili powder, and cayenne pepper. Mix the mushrooms into the

Ingredients	Directions
❖ 1/4 teaspoon ground cayenne pepper ❖ 1 1/2 pounds portobello mushrooms, cut into 1/2 inch pieces ❖ 1 (28 ounce) can Italian-style diced tomatoes ❖ 1 (19 ounce) can red kidney beans salt to taste ❖ 1/2 teaspoon ground black pepper	skillet, and continue cooking, stirring frequently, 10 minutes, or until tender. Pour the tomatoes and beans into the skillet. Season with salt and pepper. Reduce heat to low, cover, and simmer 40 minutes.

Kelly's Chili

Ingredients	Directions
❖ 1 tablespoon vegetable oil ❖ 1 pound skinless, boneless chicken meat, cut into bite-size pieces ❖ 2 (14.5 ounce) cans diced tomatoes ❖ 2 (15 ounce) cans light red kidney beans, drained, liquid reserved ❖ 2 onions, chopped ❖ 3 potatoes, peeled and chopped ❖ 3 tablespoons chili powder salt to taste ❖ 1 tablespoon ground black pepper ❖ 3/4 cup fresh corn kernels	Heat the oil in a skillet over medium heat, and cook the chicken 10 minutes, or until juices run clear. Transfer chicken to a large pot over medium heat. Pour the tomatoes and kidney bean liquid into the pot. Mix in onions and potatoes. Season with chili powder, salt, and pepper. Cook 25 minutes, stirring occasionally, until vegetables are tender. Mix in kidney beans and corn, and continue cooking 10 minutes, or until heated through.

Ken's Texas Chili

Ingredients	Directions
❖ 2 pounds ground beef ❖ 1/2 teaspoon garlic powder ❖ 3 tablespoons chili powder ❖ 2 teaspoons ground cumin ❖ 3 tablespoons all-purpose flour ❖ 1 tablespoon dried oregano ❖ 2 (14 ounce) cans beef broth ❖ 1 teaspoon salt ❖ 1/4 teaspoon black pepper ❖ 3 (15.5 ounce) cans pinto beans, drained	In a stockpot over medium heat, brown the ground beef until no longer pink. Drain off grease, reserving 2 tablespoons to remain in the pan. In a small bowl, stir together the garlic powder, chili powder, cumin, and flour. Sprinkle the mixture over the meat, and stir until the meat is evenly coated.Stir the oregano into the meat mixture, then pour in the 2 cans of beef broth. Season with salt and pepper. Bring to a boil, and then add the cans of beans. If you like your chili soupy, add only 2 cans of beans, but if you like thick chili, use all three. Reduce heat to low, and simmer for 30 minutes to blend flavors

Dorm Room Chili Mac

Ingredients	Directions
❖ 1 (7.25 ounce) package macaroni and cheese mix ❖ 1 (14 ounce) can hot dog chili ❖ 1/4 cup shredded Cheddar cheese, or cheese of choice	Cook macaroni and cheese in a saucepan on the stovetop according to package directions. Once macaroni and cheese is done, stir in chili, and cook over medium heat until hot, about 2 minutes. Sprinkle with shredded cheese to serve.

Microwave Classic Chili

Ingredients	Directions
❖ 1 pound ground beef ❖ 1 medium onion, finely chopped ❖ 2 (14.5 ounce) cans stewed tomatoes ❖ 2 teaspoons chili powder ❖ 1 1/2 teaspoons prepared mustard ❖ 1 (16 ounce) can kidney beans, rinsed and drained ❖ salt and pepper to taste	Crumble the beef into a 2-qt. microwave-safe bowl. Add onion; mix well. Cover and microwave on high for 5 minutes or until meat is no longer pink; drain. Stir in the tomatoes, chili powder and mustard; mix well. Cover and microwave on high for 10 minutes. Add beans and mix well. Cover and microwave on high for 3 minutes longer. Add salt and pepper.

Habanero Hellfire Chili

Ingredients	Directions
❖ 1/2 pound bacon ❖ 1 pound ground round ❖ 1 pound ground pork ❖ 1 green bell pepper, diced ❖ 1 yellow onion, diced ❖ 6 jalapeno peppers, seeded and chopped ❖ 6 habanero peppers, seeded and chopped ❖ 8 Anaheim peppers, seeded and diced ❖ 2 cloves garlic, minced ❖ 1 1/2 tablespoons ground cumin ❖ 1 tablespoon crushed red pepper flakes ❖ 3 tablespoons chili powder ❖ 2 tablespoons beef bouillon granules ❖ 1 (28 ounce) can crushed tomatoes ❖ 2 (16 ounce) cans whole peeled tomatoes, drained ❖ 2 (16 ounce) cans chili beans,	Place bacon in a large soup pot. Cook over medium high heat until evenly brown. Drain excess grease, leaving enough to coat bottom of pot Remove bacon, drain on paper towels and chop. Brown beef and pork in pot over medium high heat. When meat is browned, stir in the bell pepper, onion, jalapeno peppers, habanero peppers, Anaheim peppers, garlic, cumin, red pepper flakes, chili powder, bouillon, crushed tomatoes, whole tomatoes, beer, tomato paste, chile paste and water. Reduce heat to low and simmer for 45 to 60 minutes, stirring occasionally. Add beans and bacon and continue simmering for another 30 minutes.

drained
- ❖ 1 (12 fluid ounce) can beer
- ❖ 3 ounces tomato paste
- ❖ 1 ounce chile paste
- ❖ 2 cups water

Venison Chili

Ingredients	Directions
❖ 4 tablespoons unsalted butter ❖ 1 red onion, chopped ❖ 4 cloves garlic, minced ❖ 4 tablespoons dark brown sugar ❖ 3 cups red wine ❖ 4 tablespoons red wine vinegar ❖ 4 tablespoons tomato paste ❖ 4 cups low-sodium chicken broth ❖ 1 teaspoon ground cumin ❖ 1/2 teaspoon cayenne pepper ❖ 1/2 teaspoon chili powder ❖ 2 tablespoons chopped fresh cilantro ❖ salt to taste ❖ 4 tablespoons canola oil ❖ 10 slices cooked bacon, diced ❖ 2 pounds venison stew meat, trimmed and finely diced ❖ 2 cups black beans, cooked and drained	Melt the butter in a large pot over medium heat. Stir in the onion and garlic, and saute for 3 to 4 minutes. Stir in the brown sugar and saute for 2 to 3 more minutes. Then stir in the red wine, vinegar, tomato paste, chicken stock, cumin, cayenne pepper, chili powder, cilantro and salt. Simmer for 30 to 35 minutes, or until the mixture is reduced by about half. Meanwhile, heat the oil in a large skillet over medium-high heat. Stir in the bacon and fry for 3 to 4 minutes, or until the bacon is browned. Move the bacon to one side of the skillet and add the venison to the empty side of the skillet. Season the meat with salt to taste and saute the meat for 15 minutes, or until well browned. Stir in the beans and toss all together. Transfer this mixture to the simmering pot. Mix everything together thoroughly and let simmer for about 20 more minutes.

Wagon Wheel Chili

Ingredients	Directions
❖ 2 cups uncooked wagon wheel or spiral pasta ❖ 1 (15 ounce) can chili ❖ 1 (8 ounce) can tomato sauce ❖ 3 tablespoons ketchup ❖ 1/2 teaspoon chili powder ❖ Shredded Cheddar cheese	Cook pasta according to package directions. Meanwhile, in a large saucepan, combine the chili, tomato sauce, ketchup and chili powder. Mix well; heat through. Drain and rinse pasta; stir into chili. Garnish with cheese if desired.

Chili Cheese Soup

Ingredients	Directions
❖ 1 large onion, chopped ❖ 2 celery ribs, chopped ❖ 2 medium carrots, shredded ❖ 1/2 cup butter or margarine ❖ 1/2 cup all-purpose flour ❖ 2 teaspoons ground mustard ❖ 2 teaspoons paprika ❖ 3 teaspoons Worcestershire sauce ❖ 2 (14.5 ounce) cans chicken broth ❖ 3 cups milk ❖ 2 (4 ounce) cans chopped green chilies ❖ 1/2 teaspoon liquid smoke (optional) ❖ 1 (16 ounce) jar process cheese sauce	In a Dutch oven, saute the onion, celery and carrots in butter until tender. Stir in the flour, mustard, paprika and Worcestershire sauce until blended. Gradually add broth and milk. Bring to a boil; cook and stir for 2 minutes or until thickened. Reduce heat; stir in chilies and Liquid Smoke if desired. Stir in cheese sauce until melted.

Three-Bean Chili

Ingredients	Directions
❖ 2 1/4 cups water ❖ 1 (16 ounce) can kidney beans, rinsed and drained ❖ 1 (15.5 ounce) can chili beans, undrained ❖ 1 (15 ounce) can pinto beans, rinsed and drained ❖ 1 (15 ounce) can tomato sauce ❖ 1 (14.5 ounce) can no-salt-added stewed tomatoes ❖ 1 (6 ounce) can tomato paste ❖ 1 tablespoon chili powder ❖ 1 teaspoon dried oregano ❖ 1 teaspoon minced garlic ❖ 1 1/2 cups fresh or frozen corn ❖ 1 1/2 cups coarsely chopped yellow summer squash	In a Dutch oven, combine the first 10 ingredients. Bring to a boil. Reduce heat; simmer, uncovered, for 10 minutes Add corn and squash, Bring to a boil. Reduce heat; simmer 10 minutes longer or until squash is tender.

Mom's Chili

Ingredients	Directions
❖ 1 pound ground beef ❖ 1 large onion, chopped ❖ 1 (15 ounce) can ranch-style beans ❖ 1 (10 ounce) can diced tomatoes with green chile peppers ❖ 1 (1.25 ounce) package chili seasoning mix ❖ salt and pepper to taste ❖ 2 teaspoons chili powder, or to taste ❖ 1 cup water, or as needed	In a large saucepan over medium-high heat, cook beef and onion until meat is brown. Stir in beans, diced tomatoes, chili seasoning, salt, pepper, chili powder and water.Reduce heat and simmer 2 hours.

Chili Chops

Ingredients	Directions
❖ 4 lean pork chops, 1/2 inch thick ❖ 4 slices onion, 1/4 inch thick ❖ 4 (1/4 inch thick) rings green pepper ❖ 1 (12 ounce) bottle chili sauce	Place the pork chops in a greased 9-in. square baking dish. Top with the onion, green pepper and chili sauce. Cover and bake at 350 degrees for 20-30 minutes or until the meat juices run clear.

Chili Seasoning Mix II

Ingredients	Directions
❖ 1/4 cup all-purpose flour ❖ 4 teaspoons chili powder ❖ 1 tablespoon crushed red pepper ❖ 1 tablespoon dried minced onion ❖ 1 tablespoon dried, minced garlic ❖ 2 teaspoons white sugar ❖ 2 teaspoons ground cumin ❖ 2 teaspoons dried parsley ❖ 2 teaspoons salt ❖ 1 teaspoon dried basil ❖ 1/4 teaspoon ground black pepper	In a bowl, stir together flour, chili powder, red pepper, onion, garlic, sugar, cumin, parsley, salt, basil and pepper. Store in an airtight container.

Chili Popcorn

Ingredients	Directions
❖ 2 tablespoons grated Parmesan cheese ❖ 2 teaspoons paprika ❖ 2 teaspoons chili powder ❖ 1 1/2 teaspoons salt ❖ 1/2 teaspoon garlic powder ❖ 1/8 teaspoon cayenne pepper ❖ 2 1/2 quarts popped popcorn Refrigerated butter-flavored spray*	In a large resealable plastic bag or other 2-qt. airtight container, combine the Parmesan cheese and seasonings; mix well. Add popcorn; spritz with butter-flavored spray. Close bag and shake. Continue spritzing and shaking until popcorn is coated.

Pumpkin Chili

Ingredients	Directions
❖ 2 pounds ground beef ❖ 1 large onion, diced ❖ 1 green bell pepper, diced ❖ 2 (15 ounce) cans kidney beans, drained ❖ 1 (46 fluid ounce) can tomato juice ❖ 1 (28 ounce) can peeled and diced tomatoes with juice ❖ 1/2 cup canned pumpkin puree ❖ 1 tablespoon pumpkin pie spice ❖ 1 tablespoon chili powder ❖ 1/4 cup white sugar	In a large pot over medium heat, cook beef until brown; drain. Stir in onion and bell pepper and cook 5 minutes. Stir in beans, tomato juice, diced tomatoes and pumpkin puree. Season with pumpkin pie spice, chili powder and sugar. Simmer 1 hour.

Grandma's Slow Cooker Vegetarian Chili

Ingredients	Directions
<ul><li>1 (19 ounce) can black bean soup</li><li>1 (15 ounce) can kidney beans, rinsed and drained</li><li>1 (15 ounce) can garbanzo beans, rinsed and drained</li><li>1 (16 ounce) can vegetarian baked beans</li><li>1 (14.5 ounce) can chopped tomatoes in puree</li><li>1 (15 ounce) can whole kernel corn, drained</li><li>1 onion, chopped</li><li>1 green bell pepper, chopped</li><li>2 stalks celery, chopped</li><li>2 cloves garlic, chopped</li><li>1 tablespoon chili powder, or to taste</li><li>1 tablespoon dried parsley</li><li>1 tablespoon dried oregano</li><li>1 tablespoon dried basil</li></ul>	In a slow cooker, combine black bean soup, kidney beans, garbanzo beans, baked beans, tomatoes, corn, onion, bell pepper and celery. Season with garlic, chili powder, parsley, oregano and basil. Cook for at least two hours on High.

Chili Cheese Grits

Ingredients	Directions
<ul><li>3 cups water</li><li>1 teaspoon salt</li><li>1 garlic clove, minced</li><li>1 cup quick-cooking grits</li><li>1/2 cup butter or margarine</li><li>1 1/2 cups shredded Cheddar cheese, divided</li><li>3 tablespoons canned chopped green chiles</li><li>2 eggs</li><li>1/2 cup milk</li></ul>	In a medium saucepan, bring water, salt and garlic to a boil; slowly stir in grits. Reduce heat; cook and stir for 3-5 minutes or until thickened. Remove from the heat. Add butter, 1 cup cheese and chilies; stir until butter melts. Beat eggs and milk; add to the grits and mix well. Pour into a greased 2-qt. baking dish. Bake, uncovered, at 350 degrees F for 45 minutes. Sprinkle with remaining cheese.

Bewitching Chili

Ingredients	Directions
❖ 1 1/2 pounds ground beef ❖ 1/2 cup chopped sweet red pepper ❖ 1/2 cup chopped green pepper ❖ 1 medium onion, chopped ❖ 1 garlic clove, minced ❖ 1 (32 fluid ounce) bottle tomato juice ❖ 1 (15.5 ounce) can hot chili beans, undrained ❖ 1 (14.5 ounce) can diced tomatoes, undrained ❖ 1 (10.5 ounce) can condensed beef broth, undiluted ❖ 1 (6 ounce) can tomato paste ❖ 2 tablespoons chili powder ❖ 1 1/2 teaspoons ground cumin ❖ 1 teaspoon salt ❖ 1 teaspoon sugar ❖ 1/4 teaspoon pepper Sour cream	In a Dutch oven, cook beef, peppers, onion and garlic over medium heat until meat is no longer pink; drain. Stir in tomato juice, beans, tomatoes, broth, tomato paste and seasonings; bring to a boil.Reduce heat; cover and simmer for 15 minutes. Serve in Cauldron Bread Bowls (recipe below) if desired. Garnish with sour cream.

Josh's Four-Way Chili

Ingredients	Directions
❖ 1 pound lean ground beef ❖ 1 pound mild pork sausage ❖ 1 large red onion, chopped ❖ 1 green bell pepper, seeded and diced ❖ 1 red bell pepper, seeded and diced ❖ 1 yellow bell pepper, seeded and diced ❖ 2 (14.5 ounce) cans Mexican-style stewed tomatoes ❖ 2 (15 ounce) cans pinto beans,	Crumble the ground beef and pork sausage into a large skillet over medium-high heat. Cook and stir until browned. Drain, and set aside.Coat a large pot with cooking spray, and add the green, red and yellow bell peppers, and onion. Cook over medium heat until tender, stirring occasionally. Add the beef and sausage to the peppers.Puree the stewed tomatoes using a blender or food processor, and stir them into the pot along with the chili seasoning. Mix in the

Ingredients	Directions
drained ❖ 2 (1.25 ounce) packages chili seasoning mix ❖ 1 (8 ounce) package angel hair pasta ❖ 1 (4 ounce) packet saltine crackers ❖ 2 cups shredded Cheddar cheese	pinto beans, and heat to a simmer. Bring a large pot of lightly salted water to a boil. Add the angel hair pasta, and cook until tender, 2 to 3 minutes. Drain. When serving the chili, place the items on your plate in the following order: Start with pasta, then crush some saltine crackers, then some shredded cheese, and then chili. Mix it all up and enjoy! Caution, if you are not careful with your portions, you will end up with a helping too huge to finish.

Smoky Chipotle Chili

Ingredients	Directions
❖ 1 pound ground beef ❖ 2 cloves garlic, minced ❖ 1 tablespoon chili powder ❖ 1 (15 ounce) can red kidney beans, rinsed and drained ❖ 1 cup Pace® Chipotle Chunky Salsa ❖ 1 cup frozen whole kernel corn ❖ 1 (14 ounce) can Swanson® Seasoned Beef Broth with Onion Cornbread Squares	Cook beef, garlic and chili powder in saucepot until browned. Pour off fat. Add beans, salsa, corn and broth. Heat to a boil. Cook over low heat 15 minutes. Serve with Cornbread Squares.

Cincinnati Chili II

Ingredients	Directions
❖ 1 pound ground beef ❖ 1 cup chopped green bell pepper ❖ 1/2 cup chopped onion ❖ 3 tablespoons chili powder ❖ 2 cloves garlic, minced ❖ 2 (10.75 ounce) cans condensed tomato soup ❖ 1 (15 ounce) can kidney beans ❖ 1 tablespoon distilled white vinegar ❖ 1/4 teaspoon ground cinnamon ❖ 1/4 cup shredded Cheddar ❖ cheese	In a 4 quart saucepan over medium heat, cook ground beef, green pepper, onion, chili powder and garlic, until beef isbrowned and vegetables are tender. Drain fat off of beef/vegetable mixture. Add undrained kidney beans, tomato soup, vinegar and cinnamon to soup, and bring to a boil. Simmer for 15 minutes, stirring occasionally. Heat through.Serve with sprinkled cheese on top.

Chili Relleno Squares

Ingredients	Directions
❖ 3 cups shredded Monterey Jack cheese ❖ 1 1/2 cups shredded Cheddar cheese ❖ 2 (4 ounce) cans chopped green chilies, drained ❖ 2 eggs ❖ 2 tablespoons milk ❖ 1 tablespoon all-purpose flour	Layer cheeses and chilies in a greased 8-in. square baking dish, starting and ending with cheese. In a bowl, beat the eggs. Add the milk and flour; pour over cheese. Bake at 375 degrees F for 30 minutes or until set. Cut into small squares. Serve warm.

Green Chili Burritos

Ingredients	Directions
❖ 1 pound boneless pork, cut into 3/4-inch cubes ❖ 1 tablespoon olive or vegetable oil ❖ 1 (10 ounce) can diced tomatoes and green chilies, undrained ❖ 2 garlic cloves, minced ❖ 1 cup water ❖ 1 cup diced fresh tomato ❖ 1/2 cup chopped onion ❖ 1/4 cup chopped green pepper ❖ 1/2 teaspoon dried oregano ❖ 1/2 teaspoon salt ❖ 1/4 teaspoon pepper ❖ 1/4 teaspoon ground cumin ❖ 5 teaspoons cornstarch ❖ 2 tablespoons cold water ❖ 1 (16 ounce) can refried beans ❖ 10 (6 inch) flour tortillas, warmed	In a skillet over medium heat, brown pork in oil; drain. Add the next 10 ingredients; bring to a boil. Reduce heat; cover and simmer for 1 hour or until pork is tender. Combine cornstarch and cold water until smooth; add to pork mixture, stirring constantly. Bring to a boil; boil and stir for 2 minutes. Meanwhile, heat refried beans; spread evenly on tortillas. Spoon pork mixture down the center of tortillas; fold in sides.

The Ultimate Chili

Ingredients	Directions
❖ 1 pound lean ground beef salt and pepper to taste ❖ 3 (15 ounce) cans dark red kidney beans ❖ 3 (14.5 ounce) cans Mexican-style stewed tomatoes ❖ 2 stalks celery, chopped ❖ 1 red bell pepper, chopped ❖ 1/4 cup red wine vinegar ❖ 2 tablespoons chili powder ❖ 1 teaspoon ground cumin ❖ 1 teaspoon dried parsley ❖ 1 teaspoon dried basil ❖ 1 dash Worcestershire sauce ❖ 1/2 cup red wine	In a large skillet over medium-high heat, cook ground beef until evenly browned. Drain off grease, and season to taste with salt and pepper.In a slow cooker, combine the cooked beef, kidney beans, tomatoes, celery, red bell pepper, and red wine vinegar. Season with chili powder, cumin, parsley, basil and Worcestershire sauce. Stir to distribute ingredients evenly.Cook on High for 6 hours, or on Low for 8 hours. Pour in the wine during the last 2 hours.

Drunk Deer Chili

Ingredients	Directions
❖ 1/4 cup butter ❖ 1 pound ground venison ❖ 1 pound cubed beef stew meat ❖ 1 pound cubed pork stew meat ❖ 1 large onion, chopped ❖ 1 fresh jalapeno pepper, seeded and minced ❖ 3 tablespoons chili powder ❖ 1/2 teaspoon cayenne pepper ❖ 1 1/2 teaspoons ground cumin ❖ 2 (14 ounce) cans stewed tomatoes, with juice ❖ 1 (15 ounce) can tomato sauce ❖ 6 cloves garlic, minced ❖ 4 cubes beef bouillon, crumbled ❖ 1/4 cup Kentucky bourbon ❖ 2 (12 fluid ounce) cans pilsner-style beer ❖ 2 cups water	Melt the butter in a large pot over medium heat. Cook the venison, beef, and pork in the melted butter until completely browned. Add the onion and jalapeno; cook until tender. Season with chili powder, cayenne pepper, and cumin. Stir in the stewed tomatoes, tomato sauce, garlic and beef bouillon. Pour the bourbon, beer, and water into the mixture and stir. Bring the chili to a boil; cover and reduce heat to medium-low; simmer about 1 hour, stirring frequently.

Frank's Spicy Alabama Onion Beer Chili

Ingredients	Directions
❖ 2 pounds ground beef chuck ❖ 2 large white onions, chopped ❖ 2 (14.5 ounce) cans diced tomatoes with juice ❖ 2 (15 ounce) cans tomato sauce ❖ 1 (12 fluid ounce) can beer ❖ 2 (15 ounce) cans spicy chili beans ❖ 1/4 cup Worcestershire sauce ❖ 3 tablespoons hot pepper sauce (e.g. Tabascoв„ў), or to taste ❖ 1/3 cup chili powder ❖ 4 fresh jalapeno peppers, seeded and chopped	Crumble the ground chuck into a skillet over medium heat. Cook, stirring occasionally until evenly browned. Drain grease. Transfer the beef to a large soup pot. Add onions, diced tomatoes, tomato sauce, beer and chili beans. Season with Worcestershire sauce, hot pepper sauce, chili powder, jalapenos, and red pepper flakes, if using. Cover the pot, and simmer over low heat for 2 hours. Turn off heat, and let cool, then refrigerate for two days.It gets much better with time. Heat and serve.

❖ 3 tablespoons red pepper flakes, or to taste (optional)	

Chili-Stuffed Baked Potatoes

Ingredients	Directions
❖ 1 pound ground beef ❖ 1 small onion, chopped ❖ 2 cups RaguB® Old World StyleB® Pasta Sauce ❖ 4 large potatoes, baked and split ❖ 1 tablespoon chili powder ❖ 1 (19 ounce) can red kidney beans, rinsed and drained	Brown ground beef with onion in 12-inch skillet, stirring occasionally, 8 minutes or until onion is tender; drain if desired. Stir in chili powder and cook 30 seconds. Stir in beans and Ragu B® Old World Style B® Pasta Sauce. Bring to a boil over high heat. Reduce heat to low and simmer, stirring occasionally, 5 minutes or until heated through. Evenly top hot potatoes with ground beef mixture. Garnish, if desired, with diced avocado, sour cream and shredded cheddar cheese.

Turkey Bean Chili

Ingredients	Directions
❖ 2 pounds ground turkey ❖ 1 cup chopped onion ❖ 1 cup chopped green pepper ❖ 4 (14.5 ounce) cans stewed tomatoes, cut up ❖ 1 (16 ounce) can kidney beans, rinsed and drained ❖ 1 (15.5 ounce) can chili beans, undrained ❖ 1 (15 ounce) can pinto beans, rinsed and drained ❖ 1 (15 ounce) can black beans, rinsed and drained ❖ 1 jalapeno pepper, seeded and chopped* ❖ 1 tablespoon chili powder ❖ 1 teaspoon ground cumin ❖ 1 teaspoon salt ❖ 1/4 teaspoon cayenne pepper	In a Dutch oven or soup kettle, cook the turkey, onion and green pepper over medium heat until meat is no longer pink; drain. Stir in the remaining ingredients. Bring to a boil. Reduce heat; cover and simmer for 20 minutes.

Dakota's Texas Style Chili

Ingredients	Directions
❖ 4 slices bacon, chopped ❖ 2 onions, chopped ❖ 8 cloves garlic, chopped ❖ 2 teaspoons dried oregano ❖ 1 teaspoon cayenne pepper ❖ 3 tablespoons paprika ❖ 1/3 cup chili powder ❖ 1 tablespoon cumin ❖ 4 pounds boneless beef chuck or rump, cut into 1/2-inch cubes ❖ 4 3/4 cups water ❖ 1 (12 fluid ounce) can beer ❖ 4 canned Chipotle peppers in adobo sauce, seeded and minced ❖ 2 tablespoons cornmeal	In a heavy pot or Dutch oven, cook bacon over medium heat until crispy, stirring occasionally. Drain off excess grease, leaving enough to coat the bottom of the pan. Add onions and garlic; cook and stir until the onions are tender. Season with oregano, cayenne pepper, paprika, chili powder and cumin. Cook and stir for about 30 seconds to toast the spices. Stir in the beef, water, beer, chipotle peppers, and cornmeal; bring to a boil. Reduce heat to low and simmer, uncovered, until beef is tender, 2 1/2 to 3 hours.

Chili-Spiced Chicken Breasts

Ingredients	Directions
❖ 3/4 teaspoon chili powder ❖ 1/2 teaspoon salt ❖ 1/2 teaspoon ground cumin ❖ 1/4 teaspoon garlic powder ❖ 1/8 teaspoon cayenne pepper ❖ 4 (4 ounce) boneless, skinless chicken breast halves ❖ 1 teaspoon canola oil ❖ 1/4 cup chopped green onions ❖ 1 jalapeno pepper, seeded and finely chopped* ❖ 1 garlic clove, minced ❖ 1 (14.5 ounce) can diced tomatoes, undrained ❖ 1 teaspoon cornstarch ❖ 2 teaspoons water	Combine the first five ingredients; rub over chicken. In a nonstick skillet, brown chicken in oil on both sides. Add onions, jalapeno and garlic; saute for 1 minute. Add tomatoes; bring to a boil. Reduce heat; cover and simmer for 15-20 minutes or until chicken juices run clear. Remove chicken and keep warm. In a small bowl, combine cornstarch and water until smooth; stir into tomato mixture. Bring to a boil; cook and stir for 1 minute or until slightly thickened.

Lightning Source UK Ltd.
Milton Keynes UK
UKHW051240170621
385664UK00002B/311